The Impossible Rescue

THE TRUE STORY OF AN AMAZING ARCTIC ADVENTURE

MARTIN W. SANDLER

CANDLEWICK PRESS

NOTE: Sources sometimes vary as to the spelling of some of the names of places and people in this book. Where this occurs, the author has chosen to use the spelling contained in the diaries, journals, and official reports of those who participated in the Arctic rescue.

Photography credits appear on page 158.

Map illustration copyright © 2012 by Karen Minot

Copyright © 2012 by Martin W. Sandler

First paperback edition 2014

The Library of Congress has cataloged the hardcover edition as follows:

Sandler, Martin W.
The impossible rescue / Martin Sandler. — 1st ed.
p.   cm.
ISBN 978-0-7636-5080-3 (hardcover)
1. Overland Relief Expedition (1897–1898)
2. Whaling ships — Accidents — Alaska — Barrow, Point — History — 19th century.
3. Whaling — Alaska — Barrow, Point — History — 19th century.
4. Reindeer — Alaska — History — 19th century.
5. Rescues — Alaska — History — 19th century.
6. Barrow, Point (Alaska) — History — 19th century. 7. Bear (Ship)
I. Title.
F912.B2S26 2012
979.803 — dc22   2011018618

ISBN 978-0-7636-7093-1 (paperback)

20 21 22 APS 10 9 8 7 6 5 4

Printed in Humen, Dongguan, China

This book was typeset in Dante.

Candlewick Press
99 Dover Street
Somerville, Massachusetts 02144

visit us at www.candlewick.com

This book is dedicated to Jill Heine, whose efforts for human rights make her one of the greatest rescuers of all.

Contents

This map, based on one drawn about 1887, shows the key places in the Arctic where the story you are about to read took place, from the tiny village of Tununak, in the southwest corner of Alaska, to Point Barrow, the farthest point north. The names indicated in the waters off Point Barrow are those of the whaling ships that, in 1897, became trapped in the ice there.

Impossible Rescue

The book you are about to read tells the story of one of the world's most amazing adventures, a saga based on arguably the most daring rescue plan ever devised. It is a story filled with extraordinary courage, unprecedented personal sacrifices, human failings, and continual suspense.

The people you are about to meet were as remarkable as the story they lived. Called upon to accomplish what most believed to be impossible by no less a person than the president of the United States, they were thrust into the harshest and most dangerous environment in the world, an immense region of ice and snow with temperatures that fell to as low as sixty degrees below zero, a place where a person's every step might very well be his last. You will also meet an extraordinary ship and its crew. And throughout the book, you will encounter the unique and often misunderstood people who had long made this harsh region their home and will discover the essential role they played as a miracle in the Arctic unfolded.

In order to do it justice, I have told this story, wherever appropriate, through the words of those who took part in it. This has been made possible by the existence of reports, diaries, journals, letters, and detailed reminiscences written by the principal characters. Researching the illustrations for the book yielded a most welcome and important surprise. Initially, I was delighted to discover photographs that had been taken during the actual adventure. I became even more thrilled when I was later able to determine that many of the pictures were taken by one of the most important characters in the story.

Adventure, suspense, almost unimaginable heroics — these are just some of the ingredients of a story made even more remarkable because it really happened. But above all, the story is a celebration of the human spirit, one that, in the most dramatic fashion, reveals how brave men and women will risk and sacrifice all to help those in peril.

The whaleship Alexander approaches ice-filled Point Barrow, Alaska. "Never in all man's history," historian Everett S. Allen would write, "has there ever been anything comparable to whaling in terms of what it demanded of those afloat who pursued it, or the vessels in which they sailed."

CHAPTER ONE

Stranded

Benjamin Tilton, the captain of the whaleship *Alexander* from San Francisco, was in the final month of a whaling trip. He and the captains of the *Orca,* the *Belvedere,* the *Jesse H. Freeman,* and the *Rosario* were convinced that they would have a few more weeks of fair weather to fill their holds before heading south.

The *Alexander* and the other vessels were hunting for bowhead whales. The weather had been excellent, enabling them to catch scores of the mammoth creatures, enough to provide tons of the bowheads' enormous bones, which were turned into profitable, commonly used items such as buggy whips, clothespins, carriage wheels, pie cutters, and, most important of all, the corset stays that helped women throughout the world enhance their figures. It was only the first of September, 1897, yet, without warning, the temperature plunged dramatically and heavy ice came sweeping in from far out at sea. So much ice formed in the north off Point Barrow, Alaska, that the ships were forced to lay anchor to wait for favorable winds to drive the ice away.

The winds that Captain Tilton had silently prayed for came, but they were hardly favorable. With them they brought a whole new unbroken pack of ice, a mile and a half long and a half a mile wide. Looking out at the ice, which now seemed to stretch on forever, and then over the first mate's shoulder, Tilton noticed what the officer had entered in his log. "We have to get out[;] the ice [is] bad this year."

The whaler Belvedere *was one of the most well-traveled ships of its time. As author Richard Ellis stated, "In their search for [whales] the roving whalers opened the world, much as the explorers of the sixteenth century had done in their quest for the riches of the Indies."*

The weather was not the only thing troubling Tilton. He was outraged at the behavior of the other captains. From the moment they had become icebound, they had taken to gathering aboard the *Belvedere* for a continuous round of drinking parties. "This went on for several days," James Allen, one of the engineers aboard the *Freeman*, would later write. "The captains didn't pay much attention to the ice, or to anything else during their parties. . . . They didn't regard the situation as serious. They reckoned that when a nor'easter came it would drive the ice out again. . . . A few days later came the northeast wind, and oh boy, she blew, believe me! But the ice never moved. These partying captains now commenced to realize that their ships were in a dangerous position."

As Tilton knew, spending a winter in the ice meant surviving months of almost twenty-four-hour-a-day darkness and temperatures that plummeted to as far as sixty degrees below zero. It meant never knowing when the ice would suddenly move with a force that could splinter a ship beyond recognition. And that was far from all. The whaleships had expected to leave the Arctic by mid-November. None of them carried nearly enough food and other supplies to sustain the men through the winter.

Captain Tilton was determined to get himself out of this icy trap. Fortunately, his ship was imprisoned in a spot where the ice was not yet quite as thick as that surrounding the other vessels. Like most of the other ships, the *Alexander* was part of a whole new breed of whaling vessels, powered by steam as well as sail. On September 4, Tilton ordered the men in charge of the engine room to give him as much steam as possible. Then, for the next eighteen hours, he stood watch as the *Alexander* continually rammed the ice with as much speed as it could gather. "Back and forth we went," chief engineer Michael McKinnon later recalled, "and every succeeding crash seemed to us down [below] as though it would be our last. It did not seem possible that wood and iron could stand the strain much longer."

The ship not only survived the eighteen-hour ordeal but also managed to forge a channel through the ice pack and out to the open sea. "I can tell you," McKinnon later exclaimed, "when we . . . saw open water before us we were a happy set of men."

With four whaleships already stuck fast in the surprisingly early September ice, the Alexander *approaches a small strip of open water, hoping to escape from icy entrapment.*

Captain Tilton was, of course, relieved as well. But he hardly felt like celebrating. For he was leaving behind four ships and four full crews that were hopelessly stranded in the most hostile environment possible—not only stranded but also facing starvation. Tilton was aware that three other ships—the *Fearless,* the *Jeannie,* and the *Newport*—had been steaming toward Point Barrow as well. And there was yet another member of the fleet, the *Wanderer,* that had been whaling some distance apart from the other vessels. Although he couldn't see these four other ships, he suspected that they were now locked somewhere in the ice as well. He had to get the *Alexander* back to its home port of San Francisco as quickly as possible to let people know what had taken place at Point Barrow.

In total there were eight whaleships and about three hundred men stranded in the farthest northern point in America. With the Arctic waters freezing over more solidly every day, no ship could possibly get to Point Barrow to rescue them. And, as every whaler and every explorer knew, no overland rescue expedition had ever been sent to the Arctic in the dead of winter.

As the ships had become trapped in the ice, two eyewitnesses onshore had watched the drama unfold. One of them was a man named

The Jeannie *would be just one of eight whaleships hopelessly trapped in the ice, seriously threatening the lives of all those aboard them.*

When Charlie Brower opened his whaling station at Point Barrow, he had no idea that it would become the setting for momentous events that would have little to do with whaling itself.

When, in July 1897, Ned McIlhenny headed toward Point Barrow, he wrote in his diary: "For me the real interest in this trip began . . . when we crossed the [Arctic] Circle, for then we entered a sea that is but little known . . . bordering a land that is absolutely unknown."

Charlie Brower, Point Barrow's most important resident. Brower was the owner of a profitable offshore whaling station and employed almost all the indigenous men who lived at Point Barrow to help him in his operations.

The other person who witnessed the ice-locked whaleships was a twenty-four-year-old man from New Iberia, Louisiana, named Edward Avery McIlhenny, called Ned. McIlhenny's family manufactured a highly popular food-seasoning product called Tabasco sauce. He had spent time working in the family business, but early on he had discovered that his two biggest loves were collecting biological specimens and seeking adventure.

McIlhenny had addressed these two passions by obtaining a commission from the University of Pennsylvania's Natural History Museum to travel to Point Barrow to gather natural and man-made objects for the museum's collections. Accompanied by two assistants, McIlhenny had arrived at Point Barrow in 1897 and had rented an abandoned building that had previously served as a refuge station for men whose vessels had run into trouble while whaling in the region. When he had left for Point Barrow, McIlhenny had declared that "we expect to obtain some interesting specimens of fossils, fishes, birds, animals, and insects. I intend that science shall receive any and all benefit that may result from our explorations."

Just as Brower and McIlhenny were beginning to discuss the probability of having to house shipwrecked whalers, three weary-looking men suddenly appeared at Brower's whaling station. The second mate of the *Belvedere* and the fourth and fifth mates of the *Freeman* had walked sixty-five miles across the ice, a frigid journey that had taken them three nights and two days to complete. During the harrowing trip, the temperatures had dropped as low as thirty degrees below zero, forcing them to spend part of two of the nights camped out on the ice. There they faced the danger of falling into the frigid water as the ice drifted and broke apart.

The mates had been sent by their captains to report that those aboard the whaleships that had not been seriously damaged were prepared to spend the winter aboard their vessels. There was, however, not enough room aboard these ships to accommodate the more than one hundred men they had taken aboard after their ships had either sunk or been badly damaged.

Charlie Brower (seated, right) poses with his two assistants, Tom Gordon (left) and Fred Hopson (center). Gordon, an Englishman, and Hopson, a Scot, would be instrumental in bringing scores of the stranded whalers ashore.

The vessels that had taken in the shipwrecked whalers were terribly overcrowded, and all those aboard were already complaining about the lack of sleeping space and room to move about. There was only one solution. The whalers whose ships had been destroyed had to find refuge ashore. The big question on everyone's mind was, Would there be enough food to sustain the some 125 men who remained on the ships and the more than one hundred others who came ashore through the long winter? There was no hope of outside help reaching them for the better part of a year, if in fact anyone outside of Point Barrow was even aware of what had happened to them.

Although Brower knew that supplying the stranded whalers with enough food was bound to be an ongoing major problem, he realized that he had a more immediate challenge. Where was he going to house the whalers who would be seeking refuge ashore?

There were only two possible places. One was another abandoned building, in addition to the refuge station, near Brower's own whaling station that had been owned by another whaling company. It was in terrible condition and was missing much of its wooden floor and ceiling. But it would have to do.

Because he did not have enough lumber on hand to repair the building as it stood, Brower had his workmen shorten the sixty-five-foot-long structure by some fifteen feet. Then he had them use the wood they had torn away to construct forty-eight bunks in three tiers along the walls. It was far from enough sleeping space to accommodate all those who would be living there, and it meant that the whalemen would have to sleep in shifts. Brower also had his men install a stove in the building.

Even with its renovations completed, Brower knew that the old whaling station, which he and his men now began referring to as the "bunkhouse," was not adequate to house all the stranded sailors. The only other building available was the old refuge building, which, along with being structurally sound, had its own stove. But McIlhenny had interrupted his life and had traveled thousands of miles to take up residence there in order to carry out his scientific project. Would he be willing to share the refuge station with stranded strangers? McIlhenny, as Brower would write, "was here to collect birds and mammals. How, I wondered, would he take to collecting shipwrecked sailors?" To Brower's great relief, McIlhenny agreed, although, in keeping with his aristocratic background, he stated that he preferred to share the refuge station with officers rather than crewmen.

With the housing issue solved, Brower then turned his attention to the whalers. He sent one of his assistants along with Ned McIlhenny by dogsled to the ships with men on board to assure them that they would be cared for. Then he sent six dog teams under the direction of another of his assistants and more than twenty native people to the *Belvedere* to deliver a message telling the men that all were welcome at the whaling station and that he would divide his food with them to the last pound. At this point, forty of the whalemen were brought to Point Barrow in what turned out to be an excruciating sixty-five-mile trip, most of it on foot, through snow at least two feet deep and with the temperatures standing at well below zero.

Among those being taken ashore was James Allen, the engineer from the *Freeman,* who would later write, "A sorry-looking bunch they were. Most of these men were past middle age, and a couple were past 65. They had been cooped up in ships for a long time . . . and the [journey to Point Barrow] was quite a contest for them.

Among those who witnessed the whaleship disaster were many of the indigenous people who lived at Point Barrow. In the coming months, a number of them would become involved in trying to help the whalers survive.

"Mr. Denny, the chief engineer of the *Freeman,* had the hardest time of all," Allen would recall. "He wanted to ride [in one of the sleds] all the time, but we couldn't let him do that. He had to take his turn with the rest of the men who were in just as bad shape as he was. When it was not his turn to ride, we would make a rope fast around his waist and attach it to the stern of a sled. We would half drag him along. On one of these occasions, I looked around and saw that the rope was undone and he was lying down on the ice about a quarter of a mile behind. I had to go back after him — we couldn't leave him there. I told him to get up and come along.

"'I can't go any farther,' he said. 'Leave me alone. I want to die.' I tried to coax him to get up, but he refused. 'If you don't get up right now,' I told him, 'I will have to make you!' I got hold of him by the arm and pulled him up to a sitting position. Then I gave him three or four hard slaps across his face. 'Come on now! Get up or I'll give you more!'

"That man got so mad at me that he actually did get up. 'Damn you!' he shouted. 'Don't you dare strike me again!' I told him I would unless he came along right away. I put my arm under his and helped him as much as I could. We got back to the sled, but it was slow work."

A week after this first contingent of whalers arrived at the whaling station, a second group came ashore. Their arrival at Point Barrow was observed by

From the moment Charlie Brower had the stranded whalers brought ashore, he began to send some of the most skilled whalemen in his employ across the ice down to the shoreline in the hope of their capturing small whales traveling in the shallow waters. The whales they brought back provided badly needed food for the newly arrived men.

Ned McIlhenny: "At nine o'clock this morning we sighted the first sleds about four miles to the south. . . . They came at a snail's pace and not until eleven-thirty did the first sleds reach the house. Some of the sleds had men stretched on them, and all of them had as many hanging to the side rails as could get a hold. . . . There were sixty-five of the wrecked men in this lot and strung out as they were in a line a mile long, made quite a procession. They finally reached the house and none too soon, for many of them could hardly put one foot before the other, they were so stiff. Several were . . . unable to walk and at least 20 of them were frozen about the face and hands."

As horrendous as the two journeys from ship to shore had been, at least all of the men had survived. And to their credit, Brower and McIlhenny did all they could to provide for the stranded sailors. They knew that there was enough coal on the ships that had not been destroyed to keep the men aboard them warm enough even during the frigid months that lay ahead. But feeding the stoves in the bunkhouse and the refuge station was another matter. Almost as soon as the first whalemen had arrived ashore, Brower had begun sending those who were willing and able out along the beaches to collect as much driftwood as they could.

Food was a much bigger concern. Once Brower realized the full scope of the disaster, he had dispatched parties of the local folks he employed to hunt for geese, ducks, small whales, seals, caribou, and whatever other game they could find. He then began storing these provisions in the ice cellars beneath his whaling station. Brower was hopeful that for perhaps the next three months the hunting would continue. But it would, he knew, come to a halt when the dead of winter set in. Provisions were bound to run very short the longer the men were stranded at Point Barrow.

Despite Brower's and McIlhenny's efforts, conditions at Point Barrow steadily deteriorated. The bunkhouse had no ventilation, and the heat from the bodies of so many men crammed together, combined with the constant steam given off by cooking on the room's stove, created what to most would be an unlivable situation. "The house would sweat," James Allen wrote. "This steam would freeze, so that around the walls, inside the house near the floor, there would be a foot of ice, which in no way helped keep the place warm. . . .

"Much of the men's clothing was in bad shape. It seemed to me that they did not care how they looked, with their hair unkempt, faces and hands unwashed. . . . Just one visit to the bunkhouse would make you wonder how men could live in such filth without sickness and death."

Worst of all, within a short time of the whalers' arrival, all discipline had broken down, even the smallest modicum of morale had disappeared, and most of the men had given up hope. "As soon as their ships were wrecked, the Captains gave up all control of their men," Brower would write. "I thought it funny [that they] would [not] try to help manage their crews. All they seemed to want was to get shut of all responsibility, which they shifted to me."

Although Brower was successful in running his whaling station with the help of the community around him, he had little authority over the whalemen.

Charlie Brower employed some two hundred indigenous people at his whaling station. Here, two of these men pose with game they hunted to help keep the stranded whalers alive.

This lack of authority, combined with ships' captains' relinquished command of their men, created a serious situation. On October 21, McIlhenny wrote in his diary, "This morning I tried to get a gang of twelve of the wrecked men to go into camp twelve miles south of here for the purpose of hauling wood. . . . The men refused to go, saying it was too cold. . . . Every evening I go over with my book and call out twelve names in order and tell them where to get wood the next day. Generally about half of those called complain of being sick or lame or something to prevent their going. They take it as if it was a special favor I was asking. They little realize what is coming. If they don't get fuel now while the thermometer shows only a few degrees below zero, what will they do when we have fifty and sixty below?"

By November, both Brower and McIlhenny had become accustomed to the whalers' refusal to work, even for their own benefit. But they were totally unprepared for what happened next. "Last night," McIlhenny complained to his diary, "the back of my ice house was broken and a number of ducks stolen. It is rather early for the men to begin this sort of thing. They have been warned that the first one to be caught stealing food would be shot and we mean to stand by this decision."

In the book he would later write, Brower told about one of the women who lived in Point Barrow who had reported that some of the whalemen had broken into her dead husband's grave and had stolen mittens from it. "I told her," Brower would write, "I did not think they would do that. . . . To have her satisfied I had her go look at the corpse. Sure enough, the coffin had been opened. Not only were the mittens gone but all the clothes had been stripped from the body. . . . Of course the men denied everything, and while I knew they were lying, I had no proof."

As if to put an exclamation point on what was increasingly becoming a desperate situation at Point Barrow, the Arctic itself stepped in. On November 19, 1897, the sun totally disappeared beyond the horizon, not to be seen again until almost February. One of McIlhenny's assistants could not help but openly wonder if this natural phenomenon of the frozen North was a dire omen. Even the ever-optimistic Charlie Brower was having serious doubts. Somehow, he thought, he might be able to keep supplying the whalemen with at least a minimum amount of food to fend off starvation. But the whalers' refusal to help themselves, along with their dishonest behavior, was a huge concern, especially with the end of winter so far away.

Captain Francis Tuttle (front row, center) of the Revenue Cutter Service ship Bear *poses with the officers under his command, men destined to take part in one of the greatest of all Arctic adventures.*

CHAPTER TWO

An Audacious Plan

On October 26, 1897, after one of the most breakneck voyages Captain Benjamin Tilton had ever made, the *Alexander* steamed safely into San Francisco Harbor. The news the captain brought of the stranded ships in the northernmost part of Alaska spread alarm throughout the city, one of the nation's busiest whaling centers. Reports of the icebound whaleships quickly spread up and down the West Coast, particularly to Seattle, which was also a bustling seafaring community.

Almost immediately, newspapers in both San Francisco and Seattle began reporting on the situation at Point Barrow. Several of them pleaded for a rescue effort to be launched, no matter how slim the chances for its success. The San Francisco whaling companies that owned most of the stricken ships, along with the city's Chamber of Commerce, began sending a barrage of telegrams to President William McKinley, asking for assistance. So, too, did the family members of the stranded whalemen. Sending a ship into the Arctic at this time of the year was unheard of, most of the messages read, but with so many lives in peril, surely something had to be done.

Less than three weeks after Captain Tilton had spread the alarm, the sail- and steam-powered vessel the *Bear* arrived in Seattle. A ship of the United States Revenue Cutter Service, the forerunner to the United States Coast Guard, the *Bear* had spent six months in the Arctic providing aid to the local tribes and whatever ships it spotted that were in need of help. Now the *Bear*'s captain,

William McKinley, the twenty-fifth president of the United States, is best known for leading the nation to victory in the brief Spanish-American War, a conflict that took place at approximately the same time as the attempted rescue of the whalers that he ordered.

Francis Tuttle, stood on the deck reading the most extraordinary orders he had ever received, orders written by Secretary of the Treasury Lyman Gage, acting on behalf of no less a person than the president of the United States.

"The best information obtainable," the orders stated, "gives the assurance of truth to the reports that a fleet of eight whaling vessels are icebound in the Arctic Ocean, somewhere in the vicinity of Point Barrow, and that the 265 persons who were, at last accounts, on board these vessels are in all probability in dire distress. These conditions call for prompt and energetic action, looking to the relief of the imprisoned whalemen. It therefore has been determined to send an expedition to the rescue."

Gage's orders then went on to describe the rescue plan that was to be followed. Tuttle was to take the *Bear* as far north as the icy conditions would allow. When he got as far as possible, he was to put three of his officers ashore. It would be their task to proceed overland to where the whalemen were trapped. Tuttle could only shake his head. He had no idea of how far north he could get with winter already setting in, but he was almost certain that he would not be able to put the three men ashore closer to Point Barrow than 1,500 miles. How could they possibly complete the journey on foot?

The order went on to say, "The first and great need of the whalemen will . . . be food. It is believed that the only practicable method of getting it to them is to drive it on the hoof." The orders then explained that what was meant by "on the hoof" was reindeer. Specifically, it meant that as the overland rescue party made its trek to the whalemen, it was to stop at two reindeer stations located on the Seward Peninsula. The first of these stations, at Cape Rodney, was owned by a native of the peninsula named Charlie Artisarlook. The second, farther north, at Cape Prince of Wales, was owned by a man named Tom Lopp. Once at these stations, the Cutter Service officers were to try to convince each of the two men to give up their herds to carry provisions and provide food for the whalers. Once this was accomplished, they were then to attempt to get Artisarlook and Lopp to accompany them and the herd of reindeer all the way to Point Barrow.

Reindeer? Food on the hoof? What an extraordinary notion! Yet the more Tuttle thought about it, the more convinced he became that it was actually an ingenious idea. But, as Tuttle had witnessed on his most recent Arctic assignments, those who owned reindeer had come to rely upon them not only for food but also for clothing, bedding, household implements, and other items that were made from their hides and horns. How would the rescue party ever be able to talk the reindeer owners into giving up their precious animals? Gage's orders made no mention of what the rescuers were to do if they were denied the deer.

The orders also said nothing about what the conditions were like in that vast, almost totally barren region known as the Arctic, in which the eight whaleships were trapped. Captain Tuttle was well aware of the dangers all whalemen faced in hunting the largest creatures on earth in Arctic waters. He knew that in 1871 thirty-three whaling vessels had been trapped in the ice near Point Barrow. Miraculously, all of the more than 1,200 people aboard these ships had been able to escape with their lives. Five years later, fifty-three whalemen and thirteen whaleships were lost in the same area.

The Arctic was simply the most difficult place to hunt whales or, for that matter, to engage in any other undertaking. More than any other place in the world, it was a land of bitter uncertainties. Its weather could change from sunshine to violent storm, from deep freeze to thaw, and its temperatures could range from fourteen degrees above zero to thirty-five degrees below in a single day or even in an hour or two.

Equally dramatic was the Arctic's change of seasons. In May, June, and July, a colorful array of wild crocuses, Arctic poppies, buttercups, dandelions, and other short-stemmed flowers carpeted the land. Various types of grasses made their appearance. But this flowering was all too brief.

Secretary of the Treasury Lyman Gage was responsible for issuing the order for the rescue attempt.

Below is a section from Gage's official orders to Captain Tuttle.

LETTER OF INSTRUCTIONS.

TREASURY DEPARTMENT,
OFFICE OF THE SECRETARY,
Washington, D. C., November 15, 1897.

SIR: The best information obtainable gives the assurance of truth to the reports that a fleet of eight whaling vessels are icebound in the Arctic Ocean, somewhere in the vicinity of Point Barrow, and that the 265 persons who were, at last accounts, on board these vessels are in all probability in dire distress. These conditions call for prompt and energetic action, looking to the relief of the imprisoned whalemen. It therefore has been determined to send an expedition to the rescue.

Believing that your long experience in arctic work, your familiarity with the region of Arctic Alaska from Point Barrow, south, and the coast line washed by the Bering Sea, from which you but recently returned, your known ability and reputation as an able and competent officer, all especially fit you for the trust, you have been selected to command the relief expedition. Your ship, the *Bear*, will be officered by a competent body of men and manned by a crew of your own selection. The ship will be fully equipped, fitted, and provisioned for the perilous work in view, for such it must be under the most favorable conditions.

It is of course well understood that at this advanced season year the route to the Arctic Ocean through
closed to you, and bec
attempt

Beginning in September, the constant storms began and lagoons began to freeze over. Fall also brought with it the long periods of Arctic fog, treacherous to both mariners and those who would attempt to travel across the land. "Fogs are frequent and dense," whaling historian Alexander Starbuck wrote. "It frequently happens that the crew of [a whaleboat] will fail to find their own ship and will meet with some other; in which case they have no hesitation in [climbing] aboard the stranger, there to remain until the fog lifts and they can find their own vessel."

Then came winter. In November, ice in the freshwater ponds became a foot thick, and ice began to form in the ocean. Almost nothing moved in what had become a foreboding, frozen, desperately cold place, a place where, for more than two months, the sun was never seen. No wonder that, in his first Arctic expedition, polar explorer Elisha Kent Kane exclaimed, "I long for the sunlight. Dear sun, no wonder you are worshipped."

The seemingly endless Arctic was different from any other place on earth.

It was frigid, it was unpredictable, but above all else, the Arctic in the winter was a region of ice that dominated both ocean and landscape. At the very least, it made life for those who dared challenge it extremely uncomfortable. "When the cabin door was opened," wrote one Arctic adventurer who, with his shipmates, was forced to spend a winter on board his ship locked in the ice, "a blast of cold air rushed in, causing condensation which made the walls damp. At nighttime the condensation froze, and we slept in a miniature ice palace, crystals sparkling in the light, gleaming icicles hanging from the deck above, some several inches long. All along the outer side of my bunk was a sheet of ice which melted when I got into bed, so that during the night the upper part of my blanket was sodden while the bottom half was like a small ice floe."

Mostly, however, the Arctic was extremely dangerous, not only to ships that failed to leave its waters before the heavy ice set in but also to those who attempted to travel across its treacherous terrain in the dead of winter. As one whaler explained, "Any Arctic whaleman will tell you that when a man goes into the Arctic he is a total stranger to conditions every year. . . . It is difficult travelling here in the summer when there is no snow, but when snow covers the uneven land the imagination of one who has not spent a winter in the Arctic can scarcely conceive the terrible conditions which exist. . . . The snow falls dry and flakey, and even after it has lain for many months it does not pack sufficiently hard to support a man's weight much of the time. . . . Upon the steep slopes and in the mountains the same conditions exist, but even worse, for here large, jagged rocks and deep crevices make most of the country impassable."

Making matters even more challenging for those who would attempt to journey for any distance overland was the fact that even as the 1800s were coming to an end, much of the Arctic territory remained unmapped and mysterious. The maps that existed were often inaccurate.

The orders that Captain Tuttle received made it clear that no one was to be ordered to take part in the treacherous mission. Anyone who participated had to choose freely to go. That included the three men who would be asked to trek more than 1,500 miles overland in winter Arctic conditions on a journey that was bound to take at least seven or eight months and probably longer.

It was an extraordinary request to make, even of the men of the *Bear,* who, in voyage after voyage, had continually put themselves in harm's way to help people in distress. Yet to Tuttle's great satisfaction, every member of the ship, officers and crew alike, volunteered to go. This was despite the fact that as soon as the rescue expedition's intentions were made public, many people, including Arctic veterans and observers, warned against it. It would be an impossible mission, they declared. To attempt such a rescue in the dead of winter while herding hundreds of reindeer much of the way would be nothing short of suicide. Others, while applauding the courage of those willing to risk their lives to try to save those in peril, asked, Why send an expedition now when its chances of success were so slim? Why not wait for a change of seasons, or at least a change in the conditions that now enveloped the Arctic?

But neither Tuttle nor any of the men of the *Bear* would even consider such questions. There could be no delay in going, no waiting hopefully for conditions to improve. Each day brought the stricken whalers closer to running out of food. Each day brought with it the possibility of ice crushing the vessels that might not already have been sunk. The lives of almost three hundred men were at stake. Beyond that, the president of the United States himself had requested that what was to be officially called the Overland Relief Expedition be carried out.

With absolutely no time to waste, Tuttle chose First Lieutenant David Jarvis to command the rescue mission. Jarvis had begun his naval career as a member of the United States Life-Saving Service, in which he had spent considerable time in Alaska. In 1881 he had been appointed to the Revenue Cutter Service and two years later had graduated from its officers' training school at the top of his class. Assigned to Arctic duty aboard the *Bear,* Jarvis had taken part in the rescue of several ships and a great number of individuals.

During his combined eight years of experiences in the Arctic, Jarvis had learned to speak some of the languages spoken by the tribes living in Alaska, an ability Tuttle knew would be particularly important in acquiring from their owners the sleds and dogs needed to pull them all the way to Point Barrow. From his years in the Arctic, Jarvis was also personally acquainted

David Jarvis, commander of the Overland Relief Expedition. The excellent judgment he had displayed in previous Arctic missions convinced his superiors that he was the best qualified to lead such an improbable undertaking.

with many of the indigenous folks he would encounter on his expedition, including Charlie Artisarlook and Tom Lopp. These relationships were vital if Jarvis had any chance at all of persuading these men to give up their precious reindeer for the sake of the stranded whalers. Jarvis also had knowledge of reindeer, having taken part in expeditions that had brought some of the first deer from Siberia to Alaska. And he was familiar with Point Barrow, where, during one of his trips, he had supervised the construction of the whalemen's refuge station.

What perhaps impressed Tuttle most about Jarvis was the reputation he had earned for being a man totally devoted to duty. Throughout his career, he had continually demonstrated that he was not reluctant to make tough decisions; that, soft-spoken as he was, he was a most effective leader; and that no matter how dangerous the task, he never asked his men to carry it out without his joining them in facing the dangers.

For Jarvis himself, accepting the command of the expedition was an agonizing decision. His wife was far away on the East Coast, in the famous whaling port of New Bedford, and about to give birth. How could he leave her and go off on such a dangerous mission, perhaps never to return? But the lives of 265 men were at stake. For their sake, he would lead the expedition. And he knew exactly what, above all else, was required. "If you are subjected to miserable discomforts," he would write, "or even if you suffer, it must be regarded as all right and simply a part of the life, and like sailors, you must never dwell too much on the dangers or suffering, lest others question your courage."

Dr. Samuel Call (shown posing between two other Revenue Cutter Service members) served as more than the Overland Relief Expedition's physician. He was also the rescue party's self-appointed cook and took many photographs of the mission once it got under way.

The second man chosen for the expedition was the *Bear*'s surgeon, Dr. Samuel Call. Like Jarvis, Call was also a veteran of the Arctic. His first experiences there had come when he was only twenty-two, when he had served as a doctor at an Alaskan trading post, a position that often required him to make long trips between villages in challenging weather conditions. During an earlier Revenue Cutter Service assignment, Call had accompanied

Dr. Sheldon Jackson, the man most responsible for introducing reindeer into Alaska, when Jackson had brought the very first deer herd out of Siberia.

Given his acknowledged medical skills, Samuel Call could have pursued a much more lucrative career in far more comfortable surroundings. But from the time he had become a doctor, he had chosen to bring comfort and aid to people living in the most remote and challenging environment imaginable and where adequate medical attention was rarely found. As he had discovered, such service brought its own special kind of reward.

Call's selection for the expedition was especially important, since there were bound to be injuries and other medical problems that needed to be attended to during the long, hazardous overland journey. There was no question also that if the rescue party was somehow able to reach the stranded whalers, many of them would be in need of medical attention.

Although none of his fellow officers aboard the *Bear* was aware of it, Call had another reason for participating in the mission. At a time when photography was still less than fifty years old, he had developed a passion for taking pictures. He could compile a visual record of what was bound to be a unique, though certainly harrowing, adventure.

The third member of the Overland Relief Expedition was a newcomer to the *Bear*. Second Lieutenant Ellsworth Bertholf had his own special reason for eagerly anticipating what lay ahead. He was looking for redemption. Unlike Jarvis or Call, whose careers had already been marked by accomplishment, Bertholf had been in and out of trouble. He had inherited both a yearning for adventure and a love of the military from his father, who at age eighteen had run away from home to seek gold in California and had then seen spirited action in the Civil War. Bertholf's greatest love, however, was the sea. He had grown up near the Hackensack River in New Jersey and had spent much time gazing in wonderment at its waters. Later his biographer, C. Douglas Kroll, would write, "as a boy . . . he found the broad Hackensack River an expanse of unlimited wonders, and knowing that it flowed down to . . . the sea, he loved it because it typified his own young ambitions — to finally reach the ocean." Bertholf himself would later write that "the spirit which first takes a boy to sea, follows him straight through life."

Left to right: Second Lieutenant Ellsworth Bertholf, Dr. Samuel Call, First Lieutenant David Jarvis. Despite their very different personalities, the three men were well matched to attempt a mission upon which the lives of some three hundred men depended.

He was ambitious, and he was highly intelligent. When he was only sixteen, he was admitted to the United States Naval Academy. His career as a naval officer seemed assured. But Bertholf was also highly undisciplined and had problems dealing with authority. And he loved to play pranks. At the Academy he found himself near the top of his class—both in his marks and in the demerits he received, particularly for having stood at an upper-story window where he had dumped water on people passing below. Then he got into more serious trouble. During a cruise aboard the Academy's training vessel, he and two others were found guilty of having "hazed" younger cadets by forcing them to stand on their heads for a period of time. Bertholf and his fellow pranksters were dismissed from the Academy.

In what he would regard as the low point of his life, Bertholf returned home in disgrace. But he had learned his lesson. Determined to put his wayward

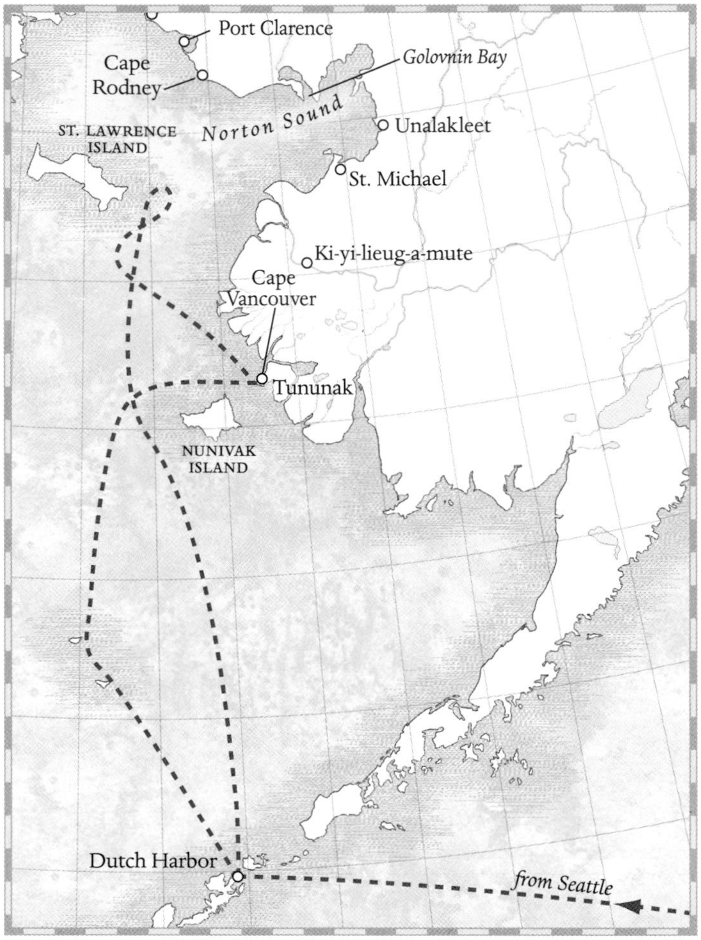
Port Clarence
Cape Rodney
Golovnin Bay
ST. LAWRENCE ISLAND
Norton Sound
Unalakleet
St. Michael
Ki-yi-lieug-a-mute
Cape Vancouver
Tununak
NUNIVAK ISLAND
Dutch Harbor
from Seattle

On December 7, 1897, the Bear *left Dutch Harbor and made it as far as St. Lawrence Island before those aboard started to see significant drift ice. Captain Tuttle decided to turn around and head south again.*

behavior behind him, he applied to and was accepted by the Revenue Cutter Service officers' training school. And this time he took advantage of his opportunity, finishing at the top of his class in both marks and behavior.

Bertholf was thrilled to have been assigned to the *Bear,* the ship that had become legendary for its adventures patrolling Arctic waters. And now, in being chosen to take part in the rescue effort, he was given the chance of a lifetime, the chance to become what he always really wanted to be—a true hero.

There was another man aboard the *Bear* selected to take part as well. He was a Russian known only as Koltchoff. He was not expected to trek all the way to Point Barrow. But because of his reputation as an excellent handler of the type of native dogs that would be used to pull the expedition's sleds, Tuttle felt he would be helpful to the others during the early stages of their journey.

If the mission was to have any chance of success at all, it had to leave as quickly as possible. Beginning on November 11, 1897, the *Bear* was loaded with supplies and with dogs and sleds for overland travel. Lieutenant Bertholf best described this Herculean effort: "It is extremely doubtful," he would write, "if ever an expedition was fitted out for an absence of a year in that part of the globe in such an incredibly short time—only eighteen days."

On November 27, 1897, the *Bear* set out on its perilous voyage. Given the challenges that he knew he would be facing, Captain Tuttle could only hope that the blinding snowstorm that greeted their departure was not an omen of far worse things to come. The ship's officers and men hoped so, too. Less than a month ago, they had been looking forward to a well-deserved, lengthy rest after returning from what was always arduous Arctic duty. Now, after so short a time, they were on their way back to the icy waters. And this time even those who had made several voyages aboard the *Bear* hardly recognized their ship. Never before had it been filled with so many provisions. Even some of the coal bunkers were overflowing with the expedition's supplies. The ordinarily open deck was crowded with barrels of salted meat. And then there were the dogs, constantly yapping and howling. Whenever the energetic, playful animals were let out of their cages for exercise, they seemed to be underfoot everywhere an officer or crew member turned.

Ten days into the voyage, the *Bear* reached Dutch Harbor, in the Aleutian Islands, off the Alaskan mainland. There, while the ship took on coal, Jarvis was able to purchase additional sled dogs for the first leg of his overland journey.

After spending an amazingly short time preparing for so long and arduous a journey, the men of the Bear *and the Overland Relief Expedition, complete with a number of sled dogs, set out on their mission. All were fully aware that because of the mounting ice, every moment lost meant landing the rescue party farther away from where the whalers were stranded.*

Before its days were over, the Bear, *the greatest ship in the Revenue Cutter Service fleet, would become legendary for its accomplishments in the frozen North.*

The temperature had begun dropping as soon as they neared the Aleutians, and soon after they left Dutch Harbor, small ice floes had begun to form. At this point, however, Tuttle was unconcerned. He was determined to bring Jarvis, Call, and Bertholf as far north as possible. And he had great confidence in his ship.

Built in Scotland in 1874, the *Bear* was specially constructed to work in heavy ice. Its keel, ribs, and hull planking were constructed of six-inch-thick oak and fastened together by heavy iron. Heavy beams and braces crisscrossed the interior of the hull. Tuttle had no doubt that he was skippering as strong a vessel as any that had ever sailed or steamed in Arctic waters.

By December 13, the captain and his officers were beginning to believe that they would be able to find a safe landing spot relatively close to where both reindeer stations were located. "On the morning of the 13th we passed St. Lawrence Island," Bertholf would later write, "and having seen little or no ice, we began to hope to be able to make a landing somewhere on the south side of the Cape Prince of Wales peninsula. In the afternoon, however, . . . considerable drift ice began to make its appearance."

Now Tuttle was concerned. "Knowing" he wrote, "that as soon as the wind died out the sea would go down and the [drift] ice would form into a solid mass which it would be impossible to get through, . . . I went . . . full speed [south]." It was a wise decision to turn around. As the *Bear* steamed past Cape Prince of Wales, all aboard were astounded to see that the ice between the ship and the cape had turned solid all the way to the beach. As a disappointed Bertholf would write, "At the time we were . . . close to the mainland, and it seemed too bad we could not land there, as it would save about seven hundred miles of travel on land. However, there was no help for it, and we headed for Cape Vancouver."

This cape was a good two hundred nautical miles to the south, and fortunately when the *Bear* approached it, there was open water all the way to the shore. A small village came into sight. Almost as soon as Tuttle dropped his anchor, Jarvis and his party rowed ashore to find out if he could land the expedition's dogs, sleds, and supplies there. "The beach at that place, at the base of a range of mountains, was narrow and strewn with a great number of rocks and bowlders, and as the snow was quite deep and soft it would have been difficult to pack our outfit over this road to the village," Jarvis wrote. "The shore was free from ice, however, and a . . . Russian trader, with several natives, having come from the village in their [kayaks] to meet us . . . [transported] the outfit to the village by water This they did by lashing their [kayaks] together in pairs, like catamarans, and they were able to take the entire load in one trip, while we followed along the beach on foot, reaching the village just before dark.

"The village [whose name we learned was Tununak] was formerly the site of a Catholic mission, but that had been abandoned, and at that time the population consisted of the [Russian] trader, Alexis Kalenin, his wife and family, together with some thirty natives. . . . Having reached the village, we were taken into Alexis's house with that open-hearted hospitality which is universal among the natives of Alaska. The [kayaks] arriving a little later, the natives carried everything up to the store, when we discovered that some of [our] flour and hard bread had been wet by the sea and was unfit for use."

The Overland Relief Expedition had not planned to start its adventure at a place that none of them had ever heard of. But it was a most fortuitous development. Kalenin not only agreed to sell Jarvis more dogs and even three sleds that were much better than the ones Jarvis had brought with him but also offered to guide the rescue party on the first leg of its journey, the difficult trek across the Yukon Delta to the trading village of St. Michael.

Alexis Kalenin's house at Tununak. Built of sturdy logs, it would be one of the most substantial dwellings that Jarvis, Call, and Bertholf would encounter in their entire adventure.

As for the *Bear,* even this far south, it was now being struck by solid chunks of ice. Having sent all of the expedition's gear ashore, Tuttle knew that it was time to leave, time to put into a safe harbor to wait out the winter. But he could not help but fear for the men he had put ashore. He was not the only one filled with doubt. As the *Bear* departed, Bertholf stood on the beach, watching it fade into the distance. "We stood on the shore . . ." Bertholf would write, "wondering whether we should ever see our friends again."

Members of the Overland Relief Expedition, fully aware of how much they would depend on their dogs and their sleds, prepare to leave Tununak on what they knew would be at least a 1,700-mile journey.

CHAPTER THREE

The Long Trek Begins

Now safely onshore, Jarvis, Call, Bertholf, and Koltchoff set to preparing for the initial leg of their journey. First, they had to load provisions, shelter, and the most important equipment of all, the unique Alaskan sleds.

"The Alaskan sleds," Bertholf would write, "are built of wood as light as is consistent with strength, and lashed together with hide ropes, so that the whole frame-work will give readily and not be easily broken by the constant rough usage to which they are subjected. The sled is from nine to ten feet long, and eighteen or twenty inches wide, with the runners one foot deep, shod with walrus ivory or strips of bone fashioned out of jaw-bone of the whale. The rails or sides are about eighteen inches high, and at the rear end of the sled are handles coming up high enough for a man to push and guide it without bending very much. There is a cover made of light [material] which is spread in the bottom of the sled, and large enough so that after the articles have been packed on snugly it hauls up over the load and the ends overlap on top. The load is then lashed the whole length of the sled with hide thongs. By this arrangement [the] sled will stand considerable shaking . . . without spilling the load."

With space upon the sleds at a premium, each item packed aboard was carefully chosen, all with the awareness that many nights would be spent camped out in a wild, barren wilderness. "Our camp-gear," Bertholf would write, "consisted of a wall-tent, stove and pipe, two frying-pans, two camp kettles,

List of provisions and outfits taken from Tununak.

	Pounds.
Tents and poles	30
Stove and pipe	21
Oil stove	15
Oil	50
Cooking gear and grub box	40
Two axes	10
Two rifles	14
One shotgun	8
400 rounds rifle ammunition	50
100 rounds shotgun ammunition	25
Four clothes bags (personal outfit)	140
Four sleeping bags	200
Two bags of mail for St. Michael and Point Barrow	75
Bale of trade tobacco	50
Sleeping gear and outfit for natives	125
One ham	12
Beans	30
Pork	50
Bacon	24
Hard bread	40
Tea	12
Flour	50
One dozen canned meats	48
Compressed barley soup and condensed coffee	25
Dog fish	150
Total	1,294

two tea-kettles, an axe, two rifles and one shot-gun, with ammunition, and in addition each man was provided with a knife, fork, spoon, tin plate, and cup. The tent was made of light cotton [material], ten feet long, eight feet wide, and seven feet high. . . . The stove was a simple sheet-iron box, twenty-two by fourteen inches, and twelve inches deep. The pipe was fitted in lengths which tele-scoped into each other, and were short enough to go inside the stove, so as to take up as little room as possible on the sled.

"Our provisions consisted of tea, sugar, beans, bacon, pork, flour, and hard bread. The beans and pork had been cooked before starting, and only required to be warmed over at meals, and . . . were thus ready to be eaten in case we were obligated to camp where no wood was to be had. Our clothing was made principally of dog-skin, and besides not being warm, was bulky and heavy, and thus added greatly to the fatigue of travelling."

Before dawn on December 18, two days after stepping ashore, Jarvis led Bertholf, Call, Koltchoff, Kalenin, four sleds, and forty-one dogs out of Tununak toward the trading village of St. Michael.

Before starting out, Kalenin had told Jarvis that the first part of the trek to St. Michael would be relatively quick and easy, since they would be able to travel over the normally smooth ice that lined the shore of Nelson Island. But the Russian was dead wrong. The same storm that had brought the floating ice that had forced the *Bear* to beat a hasty retreat had actually blown the ice around Nelson Island away. With the shore route now much too rocky to travel over, Kalenin was forced to guide the party inland.

"The first day," Bertholf would later write, "we had to cross a range of mountains apparently some 1500 or 2000 feet in height, and in some places the rise was so steep that it required three or four of us to help the dogs pull each sled up. By the time we reached the summit we began to think how de-lightful our journey was to be if our trail led us over many such mountains, since we had some 1600 miles to go and this was only the first day. The sight before us was not very encouraging, for we beheld a mountain, higher and steeper than we had just ascended, with a deep valley between."

Making their way up the mountainous slopes with the heavy sleds was a rude introduction to the uncertainties of what awaited them. And they soon discovered that making their way down these slopes was just as difficult a challenge. The first time they tried to descend, the sleds picked up speed on the slick, snow-packed terrain and threatened to run completely away from them, which would have injured or even killed the dogs that were pulling them. An alarmed Jarvis made the first of what would be many on-the-spot decisions he would be forced to make in the long months ahead. Each time they headed down a slope, he had the dogs unharnessed and had chains wrapped around the sleds' runners. Then he and the rest of the party climbed aboard the sleds,

One of the greatest obstacles the Overland Relief Expedition would face would be the rugged ranges of mountains that were part of the always-challenging Arctic landscape, treacherous barriers that the rescue party would encounter on the very first day of their overland journey.

giving them what he hoped would be sufficient weight to slow them down. Nonetheless, the sleds, with wide-eyed men aboard, went barreling down the mountain with barking dogs racing behind them, trying desperately to catch up. This must have been quite a sight in the frozen wilderness.

Fortunately, the mountains encountered on the first day were the only ones that stood between them and St. Michael. Their route flattened out across the Yukon River Delta, a seemingly endless stretch of frozen wasteland, much of which was iced-over swamps. As their pace picked up, the three Cutter Service officers became amazed at the way their native guides knew which way to go. "There was no visible trail," Bertholf later wrote. "We crossed and sometimes followed numbers of small streams, and the guide did not seem to take much account of our small pocket-compasses. There did not seem to be any marks by which to tell the general direction, for the country was level, and there was nothing to be seen in any direction but snow, with a few clumps of brush here and there."

The extraordinary skill of the guides was not the only thing that surprised Bertholf this early in the mission. He had read many books and had seen drawings and photographs depicting life in the Arctic. He quickly learned, however, that many of them had painted a false picture. "I have seen many pictures of the manner in which the Eskimos travel," Bertholf would write, "and the man is generally seated comfortably on the sled cracking the whip, and the dogs are going at a smart gallop; but we soon found that picture to be a delusion and a snare. Journeying in the Arctic regions consists mostly in pushing behind the sled, for the poor little animals frequently have to be helped over the rough places. . . . Where there is no beaten trail . . . the dogs have nothing to guide them, and one man is obliged to run ahead. . . . Natives who travel from village to village are so accustomed to this mode of travel that they can keep it up all day without showing signs of fatigue."

With the mountains behind them and no storms yet in sight, the expedition soon began coming upon the string of villages that Kalenin had told them they would encounter. The men were counting on these settlements to provide space in huts for shelter. "These huts," Bertholf later wrote, "are built in a circular fashion, and are about half underground, with the roof arched over [with] brush and what wood the natives could pick up in the rivers in the spring. The whole is then banked up with earth in the fall before the ground is frozen. The floor is made of tough slabs of wood, and in the centre of it is a small opening large enough to admit a man's body. This leads into a passage large enough to crawl along, and finally emerges into a smaller hut, built like the other one, which in turn opens into the outer air. Over each one of the openings is hung a piece of deerskin or seal skin. In the roof of the large hut is an opening, over which is stretched a covering made of the dried intestines of the whale, walrus, or seal, and, being translucent, admits the light during the day. The Eskimos appreciate the fact that hot air rises, for the outlet through the floor, being covered, only admits a small amount of cold air, while the opening at the top, being tightly [sealed], does not allow any of the warm air to escape. They do not have any fires in the hut, as a rule, for wood is scarce, and the heat from the bodies of the dozen or so [inhabitants] of each hut is sufficient to make the temperature inside quite comfortable. The cooking . . . is carried on in the outer entrance."

No single piece of equipment in the entire frozen North was more important than the Alaskan sled. Here, several of the sleds are shown drying out in a snow-house encampment.

All three Cutter Service officers were not only impressed with the unique nature of the huts but were even more taken with the generosity of those who inhabited them. "The hospitality of these people I have never seen equaled elsewhere," Jarvis wrote. "It is never grudging. . . . The best they have, and the best place in the house are at your disposal. . . . Never . . . did we pass a house where the people did not extend a cordial welcome and urge us to go in; and hardly a hut did we go into, but that the best place was cleared out for us and our belongings. What this means to a tired, cold, and hungry traveler can-not be fully appreciated save by those who have experienced it. . . . All that we ever gave in return for this hospitality, and all that was expected was a cup of tea and a cracker to the inmates of the house after we had finished our meal."

By the end of their first week's travel, all in the party had become accustomed to the warm greetings they were receiving in every native settlement. But when they reached the village of Ki-yi-lieug-a-mute, the women and children stared at them in fright. Then they dashed into their dwellings. Jarvis and Call were stunned. But Kalenin knew exactly what had caused their strange behavior.

"[Kalenin] informed us," Jarvis would write, "that, with the exception of one or two of the Jesuit missionaries, we were the first white travelers who had gone through this part of the country for many years; and, as it had been the practice of the traders in the old days to steal the women during their visits to a village, these women were taking the precaution of getting out of sight lest we should do the same thing."

With the aid of his guides, Jarvis was soon able to allay the women's fears. But he had entered the village knowing that he had a different kind of problem with which he had to deal immediately. Some miles before they had reached Ki-yi-lieug-a-mute, both he and Kalenin had noticed that many of their dogs had slackened their pace. Some were periodically falling down, obviously too weary to travel much farther. It was a frightening revelation. They hadn't even begun crossing the far more difficult landscape that lay ahead, and already he had to find replacements for the animals. Was this, he thought, going to be a problem all the way to Point Barrow?

In whatever village Jarvis either stopped at or passed through, he attempted to recruit guides from among the settlement's inhabitants. He was well aware that their knowledge of the region that lay ahead of him was essential to his continuing on without mishap or losing his way.

Jarvis had hoped to obtain fresh dogs in Ki-yi-lieug-a-mute. But the natives told him that the animals he needed were away from the village and would not be brought back for two days—a seemingly short period of time. But from the moment the expedition had left Seattle, Jarvis had been obsessed with the knowledge that he was in a desperate race against time. Determining that he had enough healthy dogs to make up two teams, he decided that he and Dr. Call, along with two native guides, should move on. Bertholf and Kalenin and Koltchoff were to wait in Ki-yi-lieug-a-mute for the new dogs and were then to bring them to St. Michael as quickly as they could. Although he felt he had made the right decision, Jarvis was all too aware that, with at least 1,300 miles to go, he had already been forced to split up his small rescue party.

Early on the morning of December 23, 1897, Jarvis and Call left the village. For the first time since they had begun their overland journey, the temperature had dropped to well below zero. To make matters worse, they battled headwinds that seemed determined to drive them back with every step. But on Christmas Eve they reached the trading post of the Alaska Commercial Company, where several traders and their families, a group of miners, and a number of people whose river steamboats had become frozen in the Yukon River were hunkered down for the winter.

Inhabitants of St. Michael outside one of their dwellings. At the time that Jarvis and his party reached the settlement, there were only about three dozen permanent settlers living in the entire top half of Alaska.

After all they had already been through, the two officers were delighted to find that they had come upon a festive scene. The winter inhabitants of the trading post were determined to celebrate Christmas. And although Jarvis had no presents to give them, he found that he could add to the simple festivities by playing his own version of Santa Claus. "Before the *Bear* left Seattle," he would later write, "the postmaster had sent on board a large sack of mail . . . with the request that it be delivered at St. Michael in case the expedition reached that point; and though its weight, 70 pounds, was a great drawback, it was brought along. As some of the mail was for the people at [the trading post], and taking it through to St. Michael might prevent their getting it until the river opened for navigation in the spring, I assumed the responsibility of opening the mail sack and delivering to the proper persons the letters directed to them."

Jarvis would have loved to spend Christmas Day with his new friends at the trading post. But with St. Michael still at least five days away, he knew he had to move on. Even though the wind increased, he and Call found that they could make good time by traveling over the snow-free ice of the Yukon River. All along the way they delivered mail to families who, rather than move into the trading post, had decided to spend the winter aboard their iced-in steamboats.

On December 30 they reached St. Michael. They had completed the first 375-mile leg of their journey. Under different circumstances it would have been an accomplishment that brought great satisfaction. But for Jarvis in particular, it was a time of ever-increasing anxiety. With Cape Rodney and Cape Prince of Wales now that much closer, the question of whether he would be able to persuade the men who owned and cared for the reindeer herds, Artisarlook and Lopp, to give up their reindeer was increasingly on his mind. Even if he could accomplish that miracle — and that was a giant "if" — he wondered if the deer could be driven all the way to Point Barrow, a distance far greater than any herd had been driven before, even in summer weather.

St. Michael, the first major destination on the rescue expedition's long route to Point Barrow, was a major trading center. The building in the center of this photograph housed the Alaska Commercial Company, which had trading posts in various places throughout the Arctic.

CHAPTER FOUR

An Extraordinary Encounter

The trek to St. Michael had been far more difficult than Alexis Kalenin had led Jarvis to expect, and Jarvis would have preferred to spend at least two or three days in the village resting for the even-more-arduous hundreds of miles that were certain to lie ahead. But from the moment he had accepted command of the rescue mission, he knew that in order to reach the whalers in time, he would be in a constant battle against the clock. That meant never staying in one place longer than he absolutely had to. But it also meant making sure that each leg of the journey was as carefully planned as possible. Convinced that he could afford to spend no more than one day at St. Michael, Jarvis knew that he had to use his brief time there as wisely as possible. "It was necessary," he would later write, "that careful and complete preparations be made before leaving St. Michael, for, as far as we knew, this was the last base of supplies we could depend upon for food or transportation as far north as [the approaches to Point Barrow]."

The journey thus far had taught Jarvis and Call that they had to have better clothing for what was to come. Their current clothing was made out of wool and dogskin, and the sleeping bags were composed of goatskin, canvas, and rubber. None of these items was warm enough for the weather they were encountering.

Lieutenant Colonel George Randall, the commander of the army post at St. Michael, helped Jarvis outfit the expedition with the same type of clothing that the indigenous people wore. The native people had long ago learned that nothing protected them better from the subzero temperatures, howling winds, and driving snow than boots, pants, shirts, and mittens made of deerskin. "On starting out," Jarvis wrote, "I had determined to do as the people who lived in the country did—to dress, travel, and live as they did. . . . I found the only way to get along was to conform as nearly as possible to the customs of those who already had solved many of the problems of existence in their arctic climate. In this connection it has seemed to me that the value of deerskin clothing has not always been known or fully appreciated in arctic explorations. The Eskimos of arctic Alaska . . . use hardly anything else, and nothing is so warm and light as their dress . . . The men's winter clothes consist of a single pair of close-fitting trousers, with the hair next [to] the skin [to keep out the] cold . . . a pair of socks, with the hair next [to their] feet; a pair of boots with the hair out, with heavy sealskin soles for hard wear or deerskin soles for light wear; two . . . shirts, one with the hair next [to] the body and the other with the hair out, and both with close-fitting hoods fringed with wolfskin to break the wind from the face and nose; and a pair of mittens. These are all made of the summer skins of the reindeer, and the whole outfit will not weigh more than 10 or 12 pounds. Over the skin shirt is worn a snow shirt, made of [light cotton], and sometimes a [second] pair of . . .

From their previous experiences in the Arctic, Jarvis and Call knew that there was much to be learned from those who had always lived there. "It is characteristic of the natives of the extreme north that they have an excellent knowledge of how to prepare for and withstand the rigors of the climate," Jarvis would write. "They seem to have no fears of it, but at the same time are fully alive to its dangers."

trousers is worn over the skin trousers to keep the snow from driving into the hair, and, on coming indoors into a warm house, melting and wetting the deerskin. A belt is worn around the waist outside the shirt to keep the cold air out, or, rather, to keep the warm air in."

Well before dawn broke on New Year's Day, 1898, Jarvis and Call, dressed in their new deerskin outfits, were ready to leave St. Michael for the short journey to Unalakleet, their final destination before heading for Cape Rodney and the first reindeer herd. Bertholf had not yet arrived with the fresh dog teams he had been left behind to obtain, but Jarvis decided he couldn't wait for

Dressing adequately was just one of the many things Jarvis learned from the indigenous people.

him. Leaving a note telling the lieutenant to join them at Unalakleet, Jarvis and Call were set to push on. But not before Jarvis, based on his previous experience, made one final preparation.

"It is always well before starting in the morning to take as much tea and water as one can hold, to avoid as much as possible a thirst during the day," Jarvis wrote. "It is impossible to get water during the day without stopping to build a fire and melt snow, unless one carries a flask inside the clothing, and this stopping uses up time. Snow is bad for the mouth and soon makes it sore, besides not being sufficient to quench the thirst except for the minute. The worst feature of eating snow is that if one gives way to the temptation there is no stopping for the rest of the day, for, while it serves to quench the thirst for the time being, it seems to really increase it in the long run, and shortly after taking some snow one is more thirsty than ever. I found that by drinking a quart of tea in the morning I seldom was thirsty until night, and had no great desire to drink unless a halt was made in the middle of the day to rest and make a fire for tea."

Jarvis and Call had hoped to reach Unalakleet in two days, but as had happened their first day out of Tununak, they discovered that winds had blown away the shore ice over which they had intended to travel and they

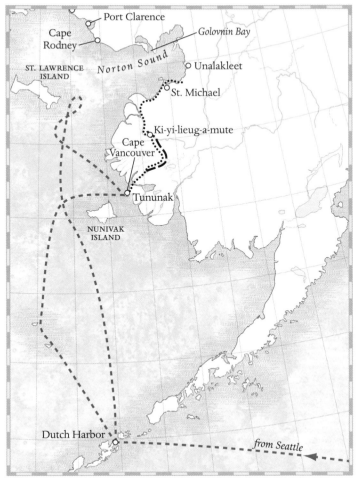

Port Clarence
Cape Rodney
Golovnin Bay
ST. LAWRENCE ISLAND
Norton Sound
Unalakleet
St. Michael
Ki-yi-lieug-a-mute
Cape Vancouver
Tununak
NUNIVAK ISLAND
Dutch Harbor
from Seattle

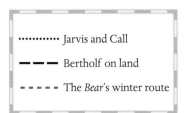

············ Jarvis and Call

━ ━ ━ Bertholf on land

- - - - The *Bear*'s winter route

were forced inland. "Our road was trying and difficult," Jarvis would write. "The wind had cleaned the snow from the plains, and made progress one continual, hard, grinding pull. . . . The next day was no better, and, though we had hoped to be at Unalak[leet] in two days, it was soon evident that we must be satisfied with what progress we could make under the conditions. We shoved and pushed over bowlders and almost bare, grassy mounds, and up and down steep gullies and cliffs, and when darkness overtook us, 15 miles was all we had accomplished."

The next day started out much the same, pushing and pulling heavy sleds over the unyielding, desolate terrain when suddenly Jarvis looked up and saw a figure coming toward him. What person, other than a member of his lifesaving expedition, could be out there struggling through this wasteland at this time of year under these conditions? Perhaps he was experiencing that Arctic phenomenon called a mirage, which caused travelers in the far North to "see" things that weren't really there.

But as the figure approaching Jarvis came closer, it became clear that it was no mirage. It was a woman Jarvis recognized. Her name was Canuanar, and he had met her a year before. But she lived hundreds of miles to the north. What in the world was she doing here?

As Jarvis listened in astonishment, Canuanar told him that she and her husband were accompanying a "white whaler-man" who had come "from the ship." What ship could that be? The Arctic whaling grounds were even farther away than Canuanar's village. Was it possible that the whaler was from one of the eight stricken ships? Was he about to discover the condition of the men he and the Overland Relief Expedition had been sent to save?

He had little time to ponder these questions. For just as suddenly as Canuanar had appeared, another figure, this one with a sled and a team of

In this photograph, George Fred Tilton (center) is shown just before breaking camp and a short time before his chance encounter with Lieutenant Jarvis.

dogs, came into view, a man just as surprised to see Jarvis as the officer was to see him. And he had an extraordinary story to tell. His name, he told Jarvis, was George Fred Tilton (no relation to Captain Benjamin Tilton of the *Alexander*), and he was the third mate aboard the whaleship *Belvedere*. His ship, he stated, was one of eight whaling vessels that three months ago had become entrapped in the ice off Point Barrow. Then Tilton went on to explain just what had happened to the whaling fleet.

The *Belvedere* and two others, the *Orca* and the *Jesse H. Freeman*, had been trapped just west of Point Barrow. Fortunately the *Belvedere* had been driven by wind and ice into a bay where, although totally icebound, it was sheltered from further damage. The *Orca* and the *Jesse H. Freeman* had not been so fortunate. The *Orca* had been caught between two immense ice floes that had crushed the vessel. Although not destroyed, the *Freeman* had also been struck by enormous blocks of ice and abandoned.

By some miracle, Tilton reported, all of the officers and men of both vessels had escaped with their lives, and at first they had made their way over the ice to the *Belvedere*. When it become obvious that there were not enough

George Fred Tilton's account of what had taken place at Point Barrow was deeply disturbing to Jarvis. Had the commander of the rescue operation been able to see a photograph like this of the Newport, *one of the ships trapped in the ice, he would have been even more distressed.*

supplies on the ship to provide for that number of men, the crews of the *Orca* and the *Freeman* were forced to travel an even longer distance over the ice to a whaling station on the mainland at Point Barrow. Hardly pausing for breath, Tilton then went on to explain that three other whaleships, the *Newport,* the *Jeannie,* and the *Fearless,* were not seriously damaged but were locked in the ice at a spot east of Point Barrow. When he had last seen the *Rosario,* Tilton stated, that unlucky vessel was lying on its side in the ice. One final ship, the *Wanderer,* had not been seen or heard from since the disaster had taken place.

Then, before Jarvis could even ask, Tilton explained how he came to be standing there. The disaster that had struck the whaling fleet, he said, had taken place at the beginning of September. By the middle of October, it had become all too obvious that, because of lack of food and supplies, both the whalers still on their ships and those at the whaling station would have a slim chance of surviving the winter. The captains of the vessels had taken an inventory of all the provisions they had and, according to Tilton, "found that our entire stock from all sources would allow two meals a day for the men of the eight ships until July 1st, but the meals would have to be mighty scant ones. This meant that half of the men would probably get weak and die, and even if most of them did hold out until July there was no guarantee of relief."

It was this "no guarantee of relief," Tilton stated, that had led the captains to make a desperate decision. Their only chance, they decided, was to send a volunteer overland as far as possibly St. Michael, where, if the weather permitted, he might be able to board a succession of vessels that could eventually take him to San Francisco, Seattle, or some other American West Coast port, where the situation at Point Barrow could be made known. "It was then," Tilton explained, "that I volunteered to go south to civilisation to get help. . . . [The captains] agreed to my proposition, and there were plenty who were willing to go with me, but I thought it all over and decided that if I failed one dead man was enough, so I refused all offers of travelling companions. . . . At 12 [noon] on October 23rd, I hitched up my dogs, . . . and after shaking hands all round, started on my trip, which I figure is the only one of its kind on record, that is, walking back from a whaling voyage."

Tilton was convinced that he was the one man among all those stranded off Point Barrow who had even a chance of surviving. "Many of the whalemen who formed the crews of these ships," he stated, "had never before been north and were not accustomed to Arctic travel. Having spent many winters in the Arctic, I devoted much of my time to travelling and hunting while the ships were in winter quarters. I was used to hardships and knew how to travel under such trying conditions."

Amazed as he was by the remarkable fact that he and Tilton had crossed paths in the vast wilderness, Jarvis became even more astounded when the whaleman described his journey to this point. Tilton explained that all of his Arctic experiences could not have prepared him for what he had already gone through. He had left Point Barrow with two Siberian natives who were members of the *Orca*'s crew, and he had exchanged guides at villages along the way.

He had battled his way through every possible Arctic winter storm, including blizzards so fierce that he had had to tie himself to his guides to keep from getting lost. On two occasions, he had been forced to kill and eat two of his dogs to keep from starving.

Still, that was not the most terrifying of the experiences he had had thus far. About two weeks into his journey, he had been traveling across ice that lined the shore of a bay. Suddenly, a violent storm erupted and the wind came at him with near hurricane force. Then the ice he was standing upon broke free. Before he knew what was happening, Tilton and the icy "raft" he was perched upon were blown out into the middle of the bay. And there he remained—for three full days! There was nothing he could do. To try to swim back to land by plunging into the winter Arctic waters meant instant disaster. Just as he became certain that he was about to perish from exposure and starvation, the wind changed direction and he was blown back to shore.

Now it was Tilton's turn to be astounded as Jarvis told him why he was there and explained the expedition's rescue plan. As Tilton listened to Jarvis, he first was amazed and then simply shook his head. Neither he nor any of his shipmates back on the *Belvedere* had imagined that a rescue effort was under way. And he could not help but be filled with admiration for Jarvis and the others who were risking their lives in such a heroic effort. But he also felt compelled to tell Jarvis that he and his companions were on an impossible, if not disastrous, mission. He was much bigger and stronger than Jarvis, and he had barely escaped with his life thus far. And he had been traveling southward. Jarvis would be trekking north at a time when the amount of daylight was diminishing each day and when the weather was bound to be even worse than what Tilton had experienced already.

Tilton saved his final remarks for his opinion of the use of the reindeer. Although he was "delighted to know that this attempt to drive the deer through to Point Barrow was being made," he believed that "it was a hundred to one shot the deer would never reach there."

Jarvis understood all of Tilton's concerns. But halting the rescue mission never entered his mind. What deeply disturbed him, however, was Tilton's account of what had happened to the whaleships and their crews: the entire

fleet trapped in the ice, at least two vessels sunk or abandoned, one other vessel lying on its side, and another ship missing.

Tilton's report of a great number of the whalemen having sought refuge ashore particularly troubled Jarvis. Evidently they had found some type of refuge there; however, according to Tilton, not only was food in short supply, but conditions in these quarters were also bad enough to have been a major factor in his being sent out on his desperate journey in search of help. Jarvis could only wonder how serious the situation was at Point Barrow. What he had no way of knowing was that the plight of the whalers was growing more hopeless every day.

George Fred Tilton's account confirmed what Jarvis and Call had already anticipated. The journey ahead of them to Point Barrow promised to be even more challenging than the hundreds of miles of dangerous terrain they had already crossed.

The icebound Newport *and* Fearless. *While the stranded whalers who were being quartered ashore were experiencing severe difficulties, those who had remained aboard their vessels were enduring serious challenges as well.*

CHAPTER FIVE

Blizzards, Reindeer, and Near Disaster

Charlie Brower and Ned McIlhenny had done whatever they could to provide living space for the whalemen. But as the days went on and the snows increased, the outer walls of the bunkhouse became banked with so much snow that almost no light came through the building's one window. The ice on the inside walls had become four inches thick, and the dripping and meltings ran down into the men's sleeping berths. Inside the berths, the whalers had taken to keeping seal-oil lamps burning. The soot and smoke from these lamps soon covered their clothes and their bodies with a black, greasy coating that made them scarcely recognizable.

Making matters worse was the fact that a number of whalemen had come down with scurvy, a disease experienced by mariners since the days of the early explorers. It was a terrible affliction with agonizing symptoms. In its early stages, a sufferer's skin became blotched, all of his joints ached, his gums bled, and he shook with chills. Soon both weariness and shortness of breath set in. In its later stages, victims of the disease developed a high fever, convulsions, and almost total disorientation. At this point, death was almost inevitable.

A British report issued in 1600 estimated that, in the previous twenty years, some 10,000 seamen had been killed by what became known as the "plague of the sea." By the early 1800s, a time when Great Britain ruled the waves, scurvy had become so widespread among those who sailed its ships that a full one-third of the British navy was incapacitated by the disease. At that point in history, no one knew that scurvy was caused by a lack of vitamin C, found in fresh meat, fruit, and vegetables.

By the time David Jarvis was encountering George Fred Tilton, lack of cleanliness had also become a major concern. More than a cosmetic problem, it was a serious health issue. James Allen, who in his observations was often critical of his fellow whalers' behavior, did offer a reason for the whalemen's lack of cleanliness: "Most everyone of the men wanted to keep himself and his clothing clean, I'm sure, and would have, if he could. But with just one stove, and that used for [mostly] cooking, it was impossible for that many men to melt either snow or ice enough for water to wash their hands and faces, let alone their clothes."

Added to all these conditions was the near-total lack of discipline that increasingly hampered any attempts among the whaling officers and men to improve their conditions and increase their chances for survival. David Jarvis knew none of this. All he could be certain of was that getting to the whalers was more urgent than ever before.

Less than two days after bidding good-bye to George Fred Tilton, Jarvis and Call, traveling first northwest and then northeast without pausing to rest, arrived at Unalakleet. There they found a mission school, a trading station managed by a Norwegian named Edwin Englestadt, and a native population of about one hundred. As in St. Michael, Jarvis had allotted himself only one day to remain in the village. Aside from the constant need to keep moving, he had a special reason for getting back on the trail. At St. Michael, the commander of the army post had been alarmed at the way in which several of Jarvis's dogs had been yelping in pain from their badly cut and swollen feet. He was most concerned with how exhausted the creatures obviously were and had warned Jarvis that he would never be able to make it to Cape Rodney and Cape Prince of Wales with such worn-out animals. Even if Bertholf arrived with fresh dogs, the commander explained, it was doubtful that they would be able to tolerate the journey at this time of year. But, he added, he had a solution. Aside from Charlie Artisarlook's herd at Cape Rodney and Tom Lopp's deer at Cape Prince of Wales, there was yet another reindeer station at

Port Clarence, which was only twenty-five miles north of Unalakleet on the shore of Norton Sound. Jarvis could not take the entire Port Clarence herd to the whalers, the commander explained, as they had been promised elsewhere. But as the chief military authority in the area, the commander would order Dr. Albert Kettleson, superintendent of the herd, to supply Jarvis with enough of the strong animals to pull his sleds all the way to Artisarlook's and Lopp's stations.

Jarvis could not have been more grateful. He could not wait to get to Port Clarence and hitch his sleds to the reindeer. But even if he was able to convince Artisarlook and Lopp to contribute their herds, he knew that maintaining enough provisions would still be a major problem. He hoped that after leaving Lopp's station, he would be able, at villages along the way, to acquire enough food to sustain his party until they reached Cape Blossom, the gateway to Point Barrow and the whalers. He also had no doubt that by the time he reached the cape, whatever food he had been fortunate enough to beg or purchase would be all but gone. Replacements for items such as harnesses, lanterns, tent poles, and canvas would also be sorely needed. By this time, he would be facing the final leg of his journey, the trek to Point Barrow over

The ever-faithful dogs haul a huge load of provisions. From the moment the expedition began, Jarvis knew that maintaining adequate supplies throughout the entire mission would be one of his greatest concerns.

what those who knew the country had told him would be the most difficult terrain under the most severe weather conditions he would ever encounter.

So, before leaving Unalakleet, Jarvis wrote out a new order for Lieutenant Bertholf. "Sir," the order read, "I enclose a list of provisions that I have left with Mr. Edwin Englestadt of this place, to be filled, and which are to be taken across the portage between Norton Sound and Escholtz Bay to Cape Blossom, Kotzebue Sound. I have engaged Mr. Englestadt and three teams for the trip, and upon your arrival you will take charge of the outfit and proceed with them to Cape Blossom. . . . You will await there my arrival or such orders as I may send to you."

Traveling with guides and three light sleds, Jarvis and Call left Unalakleet on January 5, intending to reach Port Clarence as quickly as possible. Up to this point on their journey, they had been plagued by a lack of snow, which had turned their hoped-for travel over a smooth surface into a struggle over rocks and gravel. Now they encountered the opposite problem. Almost immediately after leaving Unalakleet, a sudden blizzard dumped so much snow upon them that the only way they could proceed was to have four of the guides wear snowshoes to stomp down the deep drifts ahead of them. Even then, it was tough going. "The runners would sink to the body of the sled," Jarvis wrote, "and the dogs go nearly out of sight in their struggle to drag along."

For the first time since they had left Seattle, Jarvis began to despair. But he would not give up. Neither would the courageous dogs. Exhausted as they were, they struggled on. But suddenly the party was forced to halt as two dogs collapsed and had to be left behind. Precious time was lost reharnessing the teams. Once this was done, all the sleds moved at a much slower pace as the guides continually checked on the remaining dogs. Finally, on January 10, as they fought their way through even deeper drifts, they literally stumbled into a camp that had been hastily set up at the foot of a mountain. There they found none other than Dr. Kettleson and a group of his reindeer herders.

As stunned as Jarvis was to have stumbled upon Kettleson, the reindeer superintendent was even more shocked at the sudden appearance of two Revenue Cutter Service officers so far from the sea in the middle of January.

And Kettleson's shock turned into astonishment when Jarvis described the plight of the whalers, explained his rescue mission, and then handed over the letter he carried ordering Kettleson to supply reindeer for the expedition's use.

To his credit, Kettleson did not hesitate in responding to the order. Yes, he exclaimed, given the urgency of Jarvis's mission, he must have the reindeer at once. Not only that, but Kettleson would also personally accompany Jarvis to Golovnin Bay, where he had been forced to leave the herd during the same blizzard that had caused Jarvis and Call so much trouble. He needed to do this, he explained, because handling sleds pulled by reindeer was, to say the least, tricky business, and without his instruction, Jarvis and Call would never be able to manage it. He then offered to lend a hand and accompany the officers all the way to Cape Rodney.

It was only a one-day trip to Golovnin Bay, and as soon as they arrived, Jarvis's lesson in handling reindeer-driven sleds began. The first thing he noticed was how different these sleds were from the dogsleds, to which he was so accustomed. As Jarvis wrote, "[The deer] are harnessed with a well-fitting collar of two flat pieces of wood from which a short [rope] goes back on each side to the ends of a breast piece . . . that fits under the body.

With the coming of the new year, 1898, the Arctic winter set in full force. As Jarvis and Call resumed their journey out of Unalakleet, they were forced to trek through the deepest snow they had yet encountered.

From . . . this a single [rope] runs back to the sled, either between or to one side of the hind legs. . . . [This rope] is protected with some soft fur, or the skin will soon be worn through with the constant chafing. Generally there is a single [strip of hide] made fast to the left side of a halter, and with this the animal is guided and held in check; [this strip] must be kept slack and only pulled on when the deer is to be guided or stopped. . . . Sometimes two guiding [strips of hide] are used in the same manner as driving horses, except that they are both made fast to the halter near the horns. No whip is used, and none should be, for the deer are very timid and easily frightened, and once gotten in that state they are hard to quiet and control."

Having observed the physical differences between reindeer-pulled and dog-pulled sleds, Jarvis also quickly learned that driving reindeer was different from driving dogs. As he had discovered early on, dogsled travel meant either walking or running alongside the sled, ready to push it when necessary. Because reindeer pulled the sleds much faster than dogs, one had to sit in the sled or be left behind. "All hands must be ready at the same time when starting a deer train," he would write, "for, just as soon as the animals see the head team start, they are all off with a jump, and for a short time keep up a very high rate of speed. If one is not quick in jumping and holding on to his sled, he is likely either to lose [it] or be dragged along in the snow."

Jarvis and Call had only one day to learn the basics of driving a reindeer-pulled sled, a skill that was ordinarily learned over a period of at least three or four weeks. Concerned about Jarvis's and Call's safety and that of the deer, Kettleson asked one of his highly skilled herders to accompany the officers. Mikkel was from Lapland, a province in Sweden known for its reindeer herds, and had been raising and herding reindeer since he was a youngster.

On January 12, Jarvis, Call, Kettleson, and Mikkel, accompanied by four guides and with six sleds, set out for Cape Rodney and Charlie Artisarlook's reindeer station. During the first day of the trip, much to Kettleson's and Mikkel's surprise, both Jarvis and Call did much better with the reindeer than they expected. But the next day, near tragedy struck. While Jarvis was maneuvering down one of the many slopes they were encountering, his sled hit a particularly slick spot and ran up on the hind legs of his reindeer. Immediately,

as Jarvis would later report, the startled animal "bolted down the hill, throwing me off the sled. I held on to the line and was dragged through the snow against an old fish rack at the bottom of the hill. When I saw that fish rack loom up, I thought my time had come, but my bones seemed stronger than the rack, for throwing my head aside, my shoulder caught the upright [of the rack] and broke it . . . off. When I finally stopped the deer and pulled myself together, I was grateful to find I had no bones broken, for such a thing was too serious a matter even for contemplation." It had been a narrow escape, for if Jarvis had been seriously injured, the mission could have ended.

Jarvis and his rescue party were now enveloped by a fierce blizzard. Determined to find shelter at a village some thirty-five miles away, they kept moving. The blinding snowfall decreased the visibility to the point at which the men could hardly see one another. Jarvis, who had been traveling behind Kettleson, Call, Mikkel, and their sled, lost sight of them.

Unknown to him, his deer had wandered off the trail. Soon the animal tangled himself in a huge pile of driftwood. Then it ran directly into a huge stump. The force of the collision caused the animal's harness to snap and the terrified deer to run off into the night, leaving Jarvis sitting alone in his

Although it brought about its own special problems, switching from dog-powered sleds to reindeer-driven sleds was a beneficial decision. Here, Jarvis and Call are about to leave Golovnin Bay with their newly acquired animals.

53

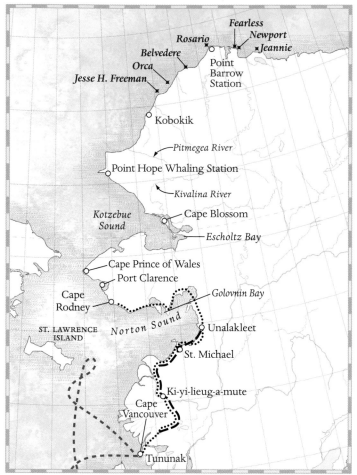

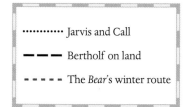

.... Jarvis and Call

— — — Bertholf on land

- - - - - The *Bear*'s winter route

sled. "It was impossible to see 10 yards ahead," Jarvis would later write, "and I knew it would be reckless to start off alone, for the others were far in advance by this time, and I might wander about all night, become exhausted, and perhaps freeze. So righting my sled, I proceeded to camp where I was for the night, and await developments. I had nothing to eat on the sled, but fortunately had my clothes bag and sleeping bag, and getting them out under the lee of the sled, I proceeded to make myself as comfortable as possible. I knew the others would be searching for me as soon as they noticed my absence, yet it seemed impossible to find anything in that storm. I thought I had been there about an hour, when I heard a faint shout; jumping up, I answered as well as I could against the howling wind, and soon was gratified to see some muffled figures groping their way toward me in the . . . flying snow. They were Kettleson and Mikkel leading my deer. I was glad to see them and know that this . . . episode was ended, for by the next morning, with the cold and hunger, I might have been in no condition to help myself."

Shortly before finding Jarvis, Kettleson and Mikkel had passed an old hut. Retracing their steps, they led Jarvis back to the abandoned dwelling, and after shoveling out the snow that had drifted inside it, they, as Jarvis put it, "made the best of this hole in the ground for the night." When they awoke, they found the blizzard was still raging and, if anything, growing stronger.

Despite the blizzard, Jarvis, Kettleson, and Mikkel, now separated from the rest of the party, pushed on. Finally, with the temperature at thirty below zero and the snow blowing so hard they could hardly stand, the three men stumbled into the native village of Opiktillik. "In an hour," wrote Jarvis, "the others came along. They had been compelled to pick their way on foot, one of the natives going ahead on his hands and knees." All of them had no doubt that, completely blinded by the snow as they had been, if it had not been for the natural instincts of the deer leading the way to the safety of the village, they all would have perished on the trail.

They were now agonizingly close to Cape Rodney and Charlie Artisarlook's house and reindeer station. But for the next three days, the blizzard raged on, keeping them imprisoned in the village. "The gale still continued," Jarvis wrote, "and by this time our patience was nearly worn out. This was the first time we were compelled to stop on account of the weather, and it was hard to think of the time we were losing with any degree of composure, but [my companions] agreed that it was too dangerous to venture out, and I reluctantly fell into line, though I resolved no amount of wind would keep us there another day." For Jarvis, it was the most frustrating period of his journey thus far. Aside from working on his journal and checking on the condition of the dogs, there was little else for him to do.

On the fourth day, with the blizzard still raging and the villagers warning him that it was too dangerous to venture out, Jarvis ordered the party back out on the trail. If anything, the blizzard had actually increased in intensity, and Jarvis and the others had to don snowshoes and tramp down the snow in front of the dogs and the sleds. In some places the snow was so deep that they were forced to dig a path for the animals. By nine o'clock that night, they were again so terribly cold and exhausted that even Jarvis admitted they needed to rest. "We hoped to reach Artisarlook's house before the night," he would write, "but by 9 p.m. we were glad to pitch our tents on the mountain side and let Artisarlook go until to-morrow. During the night I awoke to find one foot feeling like a block of ice, and found that I had worked into a cramped position which stopped the circulation and the rest of the night I spent kicking that foot to keep it from freezing."

But David Jarvis refused to feel sorry for himself. For no matter what he had already experienced, he was certain that the whalers at Point Barrow were going through even harder times.

Charlie Artisarlook's reindeer herd. Jarvis's first glimpse of the animals was a forceful reminder that his orders clearly stated that "From whatever point the overland expedition is landed from the Bear its first aim will be to get the reindeer herd in motion for Point Barrow."

CHAPTER SIX

A Desperate Request

Now at Cape Rodney, David Jarvis could not help but remember that Captain Tuttle had brought the *Bear* less than one hundred miles from this spot before the ice had forced him to take the ship so many miles farther south. Had Tuttle been able to land the expedition here, five weeks and more than five hundred miles of treacherous terrain would have been eliminated from their desperate journey.

As Jarvis stood at Charlie Artisarlook's door, he could not remember ever being quite so nervous. "I had looked forward to this day so long that now it had come," he would later write, "I almost shrank from the task it brought." He was about to make a request of Artisarlook that most would regard as nothing short of outrageous: to give up his herd, the lifeblood of his family and the entire village, and to drive the reindeer almost a thousand miles across extremely dangerous terrain at the worst time of the year. No one outside of Siberia had ever moved reindeer over such a great distance, even in the middle of summer. But he had been ordered by the president of the United States to do so. The success of the entire rescue plan depended on his getting both Artisarlook's and Lopp's herds.

Jarvis had known Charlie Artisarlook and his wife, Mary, for years and regarded them as friends. He had great respect for the way in which Charlie, after completing a government-sponsored apprenticeship program in reindeer

Charlie and Mary Artislarlook. Theirs was a true partnership in which Mary played a key role in raising and managing the reindeer herd. Later, she would become known as one of the most expert raisers of reindeer in all of Alaska.

raising under Tom Lopp, had gone on to become the first native Alaskan to own his own herd. He particularly admired how Artisarlook and his wife had built the herd up to 135 deer and how they were able to employ and train a group of young men to be expert herders.

When, after taking a deep breath, Jarvis finally knocked on Artisarlook's door, it was Mary Artisarlook who answered. Startled as she was to see the Cutter Service men, she greeted them warmly, invited them to come in, and told them that Charlie was out on the ice with his brother, hunting seals. Mary was, of course, curious as to why they were there, but Jarvis was determined to wait until her husband arrived before disclosing the purpose of their visit. Finally, Charlie appeared, dragging a seal behind him. He was even more shocked to see Jarvis and Dr. Call than Mary had been and insisted that the visitors be fed before Jarvis could make his request.

Under any other circumstances, Jarvis would have relished the hearty meal of seal's heart and liver. But he could not keep from fidgeting throughout the entire dinner. Finally, it was time to explain why he and Dr. Call were there. Jarvis knew that Charlie and Mary Artisarlook were a couple who cared much about the welfare of others. So he began his plea by describing the plight of the whalers at Point Barrow as passionately as he could. As Dr. Call would later write, "Jarvis knew well the disposition and character of those he had to deal with. He had for years met the [Artisarlooks] in the country, had never deceived or lied to them, had always been kind and never failed to bring them anything which he had promised. So he first began by appealing to their sympathy and related minutely the condition of the unfortunate [whalemen]." Then Jarvis told Artisarlook what he needed him to do, making sure that he understood that the government was not ordering him to give up his deer. "I explained to him . . . " Jarvis would write, "that I had not come with power or force to take his property from him, and that he must let me have [the reindeer] of his own free will."

Charlie and Mary were taken aback by his request, but they promised that they would consider what he had asked of them and would give him an answer as quickly as possible. For Jarvis, these were the most anxious moments of all. What would he do if the Artisarlooks turned him down? Before their decision was made, Mary pulled the doctor aside and asked him to "tell Mr. Jarvis we are sorry for the [whalemen], and we want to help them, but we hate to see our deer go, because we are poor and the people in our village are poor, and in the winter when we can not get seals we kill a deer, and this helps us through the hard times. If we let the deer go what will we do?"

But just as Jarvis was preparing himself for the worst possible news, Artisarlook came to him and stated that if certain conditions were met, he would do what had been asked of him. First, he explained, he had to have Jarvis's promise that, once the rescue mission was completed, the government would replace whatever deer were killed to feed the whalers or were lost on the way. Second, he

OVERLAND RELIEF EXPEDITION,
Point Rodney, Alaska, January 20, 1898.
Received from Artisarlook (Charlie), native of this place, 133 reindeer for the use of the overland relief expedition to Point Barrow. These reindeer are given to the United States Treasury Department with the understanding that they are to be replaced in the summer of 1898, together with the estimated increase in the herd for the coming spring, about 80 fawns, thus making 213 reindeer in all to be replaced. Should this not be done the coming season, the increase of the following year will have to be considered in the settlement.
D. H. JARVIS,
First Lieutenant, R. C. S.,
Commanding Overland Relief Expedition.

wanted to be paid the going rate of thirty dollars per month for his services in herding the deer to Point Barrow. The young herders who worked for him, Artisarlook said, had also agreed to take the deer on the long journey, but they needed to be paid as well. Finally, Jarvis had to agree to make arrangements with a nearby trading post for Mary and her fellow villagers to purchase, at government expense, whatever food and other provisions they needed until the deer could be replaced. Never had Jarvis agreed to terms as quickly as he did to the conditions that Charlie had set.

In addition to Artisarlook's humane desire to help rescue the whalers, there was another reason the herder would agree to risk his livelihood and perhaps his life to join the expedition. Jarvis would later learn that Artisarlook was influenced by Jarvis's intention to ask Tom Lopp to give up his herd and join the mission. Since his days of apprenticing under Lopp, Artisarlook had developed great respect and admiration for the reindeer expert. "If you will

pardon the immodesty," Lopp would later state, "I doubt if there was another man [other than me] that Charlie . . . would have gone with on that doubtful drive."

Whatever Artisarlook's reasons were, Jarvis could not help but be overwhelmed by the sacrifices that the man was about to make. "I had," he would later write, "dreaded this interview with Charlie for fear he might refuse my proposition, but his good character can have no better exposition than that he was willing to give up his property, leave his family, and go 800 miles from home to help white men in distress."

The Artisarlooks' herd spends one last day on familiar ground before being rounded up for the trek to Point Barrow.

Jarvis's trip from Port Clarence to Tom Lopp's reindeer station confirmed the fact that even the shortest distances on the rescue expedition's journey were filled with their own particular challenges.

CHAPTER SEVEN

Another Agonizing Decision

Obtaining Artisarlook's herd and his services was a huge accomplishment. But it in no way guaranteed that Jarvis would have the same success with Tom Lopp. And as anxious as he was to move on to Cape Prince of Wales, he realized that he was once again running out of food and needed to make a hasty trip back to Port Clarence, where he could purchase supplies. Jarvis decided that, after obtaining these provisions, he would leave for Lopp's directly, taking Artisarlook with him to help navigate over the particularly treacherous route between Port Clarence and Cape Prince of Wales. Dr. Call was to stay behind at Cape Rodney to help Artisarlook's herders round up their reindeer and move them immediately to Lopp's station.

Despite the numbing cold and the often blinding snow that refused to let up, Jarvis and his companions, including Kettleson and Mikkel, made it to Port Clarence in just two days. After purchasing the needed food, Jarvis then bid good-bye to Kettleson and Mikkel, thanking them profusely for all they had voluntarily contributed to the expedition. On January 23, he and Artisarlook set out for Cape Prince of Wales.

In distance, the trip to Lopp's reindeer station was much shorter than most of the legs of the rescue mission's journey. But as Jarvis later stated, "I think the 50 miles from Port Clarence to Cape Prince of Wales, the most trying and fearful of all I experienced on the expedition."

When Jarvis and Artisarlook left Port Clarence, they were accompanied by two helpers who were familiar with the bluff-lined route along the coast leading to the cape. But less than halfway out, with, as Jarvis wrote, "the thermometer −30° and the blizzard still blowing," one of the men suddenly stated that his gun had fallen off the sled and he was going back to retrieve it. He never returned. Jarvis and Artisarlook were forced to continue on with just one remaining guide over ice so jagged and piled so high that their heavy sled kept capsizing. With the snow pounding down upon them, Jarvis and his companions were continually forced to lie down on either side of the capsized sled and use their legs and feet as fulcrums to raise it high enough to be righted.

It was exhausting work, and, more than at any time in the journey, Jarvis found himself totally drained. "About 8 o'clock I was completely played out and willing to camp," he wrote. "But Artisarlook said 'no,' it was too cold to camp without wood, and, as the ice we were on was in danger of breaking off from the shore any minute, it was necessary that we get beyond the line of bluffs before stopping. In the darkness I stepped through a crack in the ice, and my leg to the knee was immediately one mass of ice. I was now compelled to go on to some place where my foot gear could be dried, and, though almost ready to drop where I was, I had to keep on, for to stop, meant to freeze."

Jarvis was now even more concerned than when he had crashed into the fish rack or when his deer had bolted, stranding him on the trail. The Arctic was filled with stories of travelers who, in similar circumstances, had lost a leg or had even perished. He had to find a place, any place, where he could dry out. Fortunately, luck was with him.

"Pushing and lifting our sled, and urging the dogs [on]," Jarvis later recounted, "we dragged along until midnight, when we came to a house, high up on the shore. . . . Though it turned out to be a horrible place, no palace could have been more welcome. It was a small hut, about 10 by 12, and 5 feet high, and 15 people were already sleeping there. It was most filthy and the worst house I have seen in all my Alaskan experience; but I was too tired then to care for that, too tired even to eat; and though I had had nothing but

The expedition found that traveling along the Arctic shoreline was particularly difficult. The terrain was a combination of bare, rough gravel where the snow had worn away, thick chunks of ice, and snow that had slid down from the mountains.

a couple of crackers since morning, I was quite satisfied to take off my wet clothing, crawl into my bag, and sleep."

In the morning, after hastily thanking the inhabitants of the hut, they moved on and soon found a village where they were able to get the first decent meal they had had since leaving Port Clarence. Upon leaving the village, they encountered conditions that Jarvis would vividly describe. "I thought the ice we recently passed over had made a rough road," he would write, "but this was even worse, for here were all the crushings of the [sea] shoved up against the mountains . . . and over this kind of ice we had to make our way. Darkness set in long before we had come to the worst of it, and a faint moon gave too little light for such a road. It was a continuous jumble of dogs, sleds, men, and ice—particularly ice—and it would be hard to tell which suffered most, men or dogs. Once, in helping the sled over a particularly bad place, I was thrown 8 or 9 feet down a slide, landing on the back of my head with the sled on top of me. Though the mercury was -30°, I was wet through with perspiration from the violence of the work." With the temperature standing so low, remaining outdoors covered in sweat was extremely dangerous. Fortunately, they were now only a few miles from the reindeer station, and with their

Tom Lopp at the time he agreed to drive the reindeer herd to Point Barrow. Before his days in the frozen North were over, Lopp would become recognized as one of the greatest of all Arctic heroes.

sleds racked and broken, their dogs played out and scarcely able to move, they reached Tom Lopp's house.

For the second time in less than a week, David Jarvis found himself about to make an audacious request of someone without whose help the rescue mission might well be doomed. Now he was even more nervous than when he had stood before Charlie Artisarlook's door. Jarvis fully agreed with those who had planned the rescue effort that Lopp's participation was paramount to any chance of success the expedition might have. Secretary Gage's orders had, in fact, specifically stated the necessity of convincing Lopp to take part in the mission. "Mr. Lopp," Gage had stated, "is to take charge of [the entire] herd and make all necessary arrangements. . . . Mr. Lopp must be fully impressed with the importance of the work at hand, and with the necessity of bending every energy to its speedy accomplishment."

Jarvis concurred. Lopp, he would write, "was indispensable. His capability of handling natives, his knowledge of them and the reindeer, was far above that of any one in the country." Lopp had been among the very first to realize how important reindeer could be to the well-being of the native population when the first deer were brought from Siberia. And from the beginning of this government-sponsored program, it was Lopp who had trained the reindeer to draw sleds and to carry supplies on their backs. In the process, he had also trained more than thirty-five young herders and drivers. As one organization devoted to the promotion of reindeer would state, "The early successes of Eskimo involvement with reindeer are more attributable to the efforts of [Tom] Lopp than to any other single individual. . . . The future of reindeer as a native resource clearly rested upon Lopp's capacities to interpret and clarify in the Native tongue the meaning of this new form of wealth."

Even more than promoting the use of the deer, Lopp was concerned with the welfare of the people. Both he and his wife, Ellen, were missionaries and teachers. Both had devoted themselves to learning the local language as well as the beliefs, customs, and ways of doing things. And, unlike most non-

natives, they both realized that they had as much to learn from the indigenous people as they had to teach them. For the natives at Cape Prince of Wales and to many who lived well beyond, the man who was a reindeer expert, teacher, and missionary was not known as Tom Lopp; they called him "Tom Gorrah," or "Tom, the good man."

When the Lopps answered the unexpected knock on their door and saw the man dressed from head to toe in skins, they were certain that someone they did not know from a nearby village had come calling. Only when Jarvis removed the wide scarf that covered his face did Tom Lopp recognize him as one of the officers of the *Bear,* which had made many routine stops at Cape Prince of Wales. Then, before he could invite Jarvis into the house, Lopp noticed Artisarlook standing behind him. Immediately, Lopp knew that something serious was afoot. Why else would Artisarlook have traveled so far from home, especially at this treacherous time of year?

There were many sacrifices attached to the Lopps giving up their reindeer. Many of the indigenous people who worked with the animals had become extremely fond of them.

Among those Tom Lopp employed were a number of people from a region that spread across Finland and Sweden called Lapland. Known both for their reindeer-herding skills and the distinctive hats they wore, several of the Laplanders agreed to accompany Lopp's herd to Point Barrow.

As soon as the two visitors were seated inside and even before Lopp could ask any questions, Jarvis launched into an explanation of how he had made his way from Seattle to Cape Prince of Wales, what his mission was, and what he desperately hoped Lopp, like Artisarlook, would do to help him. He also told Lopp that he was aware that Lopp owned half of the reindeer at his station and that the other half were owned by the American Missionary Association, which left it up to Lopp to make all decisions regarding the deer. Then, taking a deep breath, Jarvis concluded by stating that, for the sake of the stricken whalers, he needed the entire herd.

For his part, Lopp was shaken not only by what Jarvis had asked of him but also by how exhausted both the officer and Artisarlook appeared. The first thing to be done, he stated, was to have both of them sent to bed. Accommodations, Lopp stated, would also be made for Dr. Call, who had just arrived with Artisarlook's herd and herders.

For Tom and Ellen Lopp, it would be a sleepless night. They both knew that, aside from the economic hardships that giving up the deer would entail, there were good reasons for turning Jarvis down. For starters, there was really no way of knowing how long Tom would be gone—four months? five months? even longer?—from his wife and four children, all under the age of six. And both Tom and Ellen were aware of the dangers involved. Point Barrow was more than seven hundred miles away. Driving a herd of more than four hundred reindeer over the snow-filled mountains and across frozen bodies of water had to be one of the greatest challenges that anyone in the Arctic had ever faced.

Still, both Tom and Ellen had to agree that there were compelling reasons for saying yes to Jarvis. Tom was the most devoted of all those who wanted the government's program of supplying reindeer to the indigenous people to flourish. What would be a better demonstration of the value of the program than the success of the rescue mission? And the Lopps did not question the expedition's motives to risk so much to try to save so many men in peril.

By the time the long night was over, the Lopps had decided. The deer would be given up. Lopp would lead the combined herds to Point Barrow. But, as had been the case with Artisarlook, he would do so only if certain conditions were met. Jarvis would have to give the Lopps a written promise that the deer and all the fawns that were yet to be born would be replaced. Jarvis would also have to pledge that the government would pay Tom $150 a month, and that the herders he intended to take with him would be paid one dollar a day for their services.

Lopp's commitment was an enormous sacrifice. As Tom would later write, "You can imagine at what cost this decision was made—separation of family . . . loss of deer, and breaking our plans for this year and next. But it was an errand of mercy and we were glad to have an opportunity to show . . . that our government cared . . . and would go to great expense to save [those] in distress."

OVERLAND RELIEF EXPEDITION,
Cape Prince of Wales, Alaska, January 25, 1898.

Received from Mr. W. W. Lopp, representing the American Missionary Association, 292 reindeer for the use of the overland relief expedition to Point Barrow, Alaska.

These reindeer are given to the United States Treasury Department with the understanding that they are to be replaced in the summer of 1898, together with the estimated increase in the herd for the coming season, about 140 fawns, thus making 432 reindeer in all to be replaced.

Should this not be done the coming season, the increase of the following year will have to be considered in the settlement.

D. H. JARVIS,
First Lieutenant, R. C. S.,
Commanding Overland Relief Expedition.

For a man with no previous Arctic experience, Lieutenant Ellsworth Bertholf had been given a daunting task — traveling without any Cutter Service companion over hundreds of miles of wilderness.

CHAPTER EIGHT

Bertholf Battles the Odds

Thanks to Tom Lopp and Charlie Artisarlook, two extraordinary and compassionate men with a particular skill and a commodity that they were willing to share, the components of the race to save the whalers were beginning to come together. The mission's leaders had managed thus far to acquire enough food to keep them going. They had had frightening mishaps, but no member of the expedition had been seriously injured. With difficulty, they had managed to replace worn-out dogs and damaged sleds. Perhaps most remarkable of all, they had not once gotten lost while traveling in winter Arctic conditions over territory often unfamiliar even to the guides.

But there was another piece of Jarvis's plan that had yet to fall into place and remained unknown. What had happened to Lieutenant Bertholf? Jarvis had seen him more than a month ago when they had parted ways in Ki-yi-lieug-a-mute. Had Bertholf been able to make it to Unalakleet, where Jarvis had left the note for him giving him new orders? Was he on his way to Cape Blossom with the supplies that Jarvis knew he would desperately need if he was able to get that far?

On December 22, 1897, Bertholf, Koltchoff, and Kalenin, with a young boy serving as a guide, had headed out of Ki-yi-lieug-a-mute with the fresh dogs that Jarvis had asked them to acquire there. Now that they were separated from Jarvis and Call, it was Bertholf's first command of an Arctic mission on his own.

Years after his great Arctic adventure had ended, Lieutenant Bertholf, like all those who had taken part in the Overland Relief Expedition, would never forget the indispensable role that the dogs played in the rescue effort.

He would have to make all the difficult decisions for his party as they traveled over the treacherous landscape on the route to St. Michael. He had volunteered for the expedition out of a desire to do something both important and heroic, and here was his first chance. He would do everything he could to reach St. Michael in time to catch up with Jarvis and Dr. Call to deliver the dogs to them.

"We were off as soon as there was light enough to see," Bertholf wrote. "As we approached the Yukon . . . we scared up several flocks of ptarmigan, or Arctic grouse—the first game I had seen in the country. As I only had a rifle, Jarvis having taken the shot-gun, I was unable to obtain any, for these birds are perfectly white in the winter, and very hard to distinguish against the background of snow. As Jarvis had left me without a thermometer, I had nothing but my feelings to give me any idea of the degree of cold. The day [Jarvis, Call, and I] separated, the mercury registered 23 degrees above zero, and although some days seemed to be colder than others, I attributed that fact to the rising of the wind. Judge my surprise, then, at finding, when we reached [the next village], that the thermometer registered 15 degrees below zero. Of course I knew it was colder than when we started, but traveling daily in the open air we had not felt the gradual change. As soon as I saw what the thermometer had to say, I began to feel cold."

Two days later, on December 24, Bertholf and his companions arrived at Kogerchtehmute. The trek across the thin-crusted snow had taken a toll on the dogs' feet, cutting them so badly that the animals left a bloody trail behind them. As Bertholf would later write, "Under ordinary circumstances when the dogs' feet become sore in this manner it is best to halt for a few days and allow them a rest, for the cuts seem to heal very quickly in this climate."

But these were not ordinary circumstances. Resting for a few days was out of the question. Fortunately, Kalenin had a solution. He asked the women in the village to make "boots" for the dogs by sewing pieces of cloth together and tying them to the dogs' feet. It was an inspired idea, but it wasn't accomplished the way Kalenin had envisioned. The previous day, one of the natives in the village had died. According to their tradition, no work was to be done during the four days following a death. The men on the rescue mission realized the importance of this custom after they tried and failed to persuade the women to help them. Knowing that they had to keep moving on, Bertholf and Kalenin made the boots themselves, and the party departed for the village of Chukwoktulik, where they arrived on Christmas Day.

Knowing that there was no time to dawdle, Bertholf, Kalenin, and their companions left Chukwoktulik on December 26, determined to make it all the way to St. Michael as quickly as possible. But serious trouble lay ahead. Two days out, Kalenin began complaining of a cold. He also had severe pains in his side. At first, neither the Russian nor Bertholf thought much about it. As Bertholf would later recount, "I was not enough of a doctor to understand what was his trouble, and besides, I had no medicines with me." To Bertholf's alarm, Kalenin's condition grew so much worse that he was soon unable to walk and had to be carried on one of the sleds. As if this was not enough, the young native guide had taken a fall and had developed a bad sore on his knee. He too found himself unable to walk and was placed upon a sled. Now, only Bertholf and Koltchoff were left to keep running ahead of the four sleds and teams of dogs. Bertholf knew that there were no more villages before

St. Michael, and with the snow coming down harder than ever, he was facing a desperate situation. As much as he fought it, he could not completely dismiss the thought that, after all that he had already been through and with so many miles still to go, his role in the great rescue attempt might be about to end in disaster somewhere on a barren, frozen trail.

Still Bertholf pushed on, and on December 31, 1897, just as he was truly beginning to despair, a huge object loomed incongruously ahead of him. It was the abandoned steamboat *Healy*, locked solidly in a frozen canal. Carefully moving Kalenin and the native guide aboard the vessel, Bertholf and Koltchoff found lifesaving refuge for the night. The next day, with the Russian and the Alaskan guide once again aboard the sled, they managed to travel the final twelve miles to St. Michael.

It was January 1, 1898. But, for Bertholf, it was hardly a propitious beginning of a new year. He had struggled mightily to reach St. Michael with the fresh dogs for Jarvis and Call before his fellow officers arrived there. But when he entered the village, he was told that he had missed them by only a few hours. Bertholf could not have been more disappointed. Despite all the delays he had suffered, he had come so agonizingly close. His first inclination was to chase after the two men, but he had an even deeper concern when Kalenin's condition worsened.

Fortunately, there was a doctor in the village and it did not take him long to determine that the Russian had a severe case of pneumonia. So severe, in fact, that after immediately being put to bed, Kalenin remained at St. Michael under the doctor's care for three full months. He wasn't able to return to his own home at Tununak until April. Bertholf had grown increasingly fond of the man with whom he had traveled so many miles since he, Jarvis, and Dr. Call had first come ashore. Moreover, given all that Kalenin had done, Bertholf felt responsible for him. "As Alexis had been very faithful and his illness was undoubtedly due to exposure while in the service of the expedition," Bertholf would write, "I considered it my duty to see that he was properly cared for, and before I left St. Michael I gave an order to the agent of the Alaska Commercial Company at that place to furnish nurses for Alexis, and whatever else [the doctor] considered necessary to further his recovery."

Reduced to having only two teams, Bertholf's arduous journey was made even more difficult by the fact that his route out of St. Michael took him along a landscape where huge mounds of ice had formed.

Kalenin was not the only one that Bertholf was obliged to leave behind. Koltchoff had agreed to accompany the expedition as far as St. Michael. Now that they were there, it was time to part ways with the man who, like Alexis Kalenin, had served Bertholf so well.

Having bid farewell to Koltchoff and having done all he could for Kalenin, Bertholf was anxious to move on to Unalakleet, where he hoped he might at last catch up with Jarvis and Dr. Call. But agonizing as it was, he knew that he would have to delay his departure until the cuts on his dogs' feet, which had opened up again on the trek to St. Michael, were healed. To his increased frustration, it was not until January 6 that he felt that the dogs were fit enough to take him to Unalakleet. There were now only enough healthy dogs to make up two teams, one for himself and one owned by the guide he was able to hire to replace the young man whose knee was still not fully healed. "Although [Unalakleet] is but sixty miles from [St. Michael]," Bertholf would write, "it took us three days to make the trip, for the road led along the shore, where the ice had shelved and piled up, making an exceedingly rough and hummocky trail. Imagine a road strewn with rocks and boulders of all sizes, packed close together, and some idea of our trail will be gained. Our progress was necessarily slow, as the sled required constant watching and guiding to keep it from overturning, which, however, it did very frequently, despite our best efforts, and the next three days were very fatiguing; but we finally pulled into [Unalakleet] on the evening of the 8th, without any serious mishaps. We passed two natives, however, on the way, who were packing their load on their backs, their sled having been broken by the difficult trail."

Only a few hours out of St. Michael, Bertholf was startled to see another team coming toward him. It was the same *Belvedere's* mate, George Fred Tilton, who earlier had encountered Jarvis and Dr. Call. Bertholf was astounded to learn that Tilton was trying to make it all the way to San Francisco. But it was clear to both men that neither had time for lengthy discussion, and after wishing each other luck, they continued traveling on, each convinced the other would not be able to reach his goal, each hoping that somehow he was wrong.

When he finally reached Unalakleet, Bertholf was again disappointed to find that he had failed to catch up with Jarvis and Dr. Call. What he was not prepared for, however, was the fresh set of orders that Jarvis had left behind for him. He was not to join up with his fellow officers. Instead, he was to carry out a separate mission of transporting one thousand pounds of provisions more than five hundred miles to Cape Blossom. It was a daunting assignment. He had just lost the help of two very capable men. What would he do if he could not replace them? But Bertholf could not help but be proud of the fact that Jarvis had developed enough faith in him to trust him to carry out a mission so vital to the success of the entire rescue effort.

As Bertholf quickly learned, it was an assignment even more challenging than his commander had realized, for Jarvis had greatly underestimated the load Bertholf would need to carry. He had forgotten to figure in the more than three hundred pounds of supplies that Bertholf and those who accompanied him would also have to take along to sustain themselves on the long, arduous journey. And then there was the more than three hundred pounds of fish that would be needed to feed the dogs along the way. All told, Bertholf would not, as Jarvis had indicated, be transporting one thousand pounds of provisions for hundreds of miles. He and his dogs would be carrying more than sixteen hundred pounds of supplies.

Under any circumstances, it would have been an incredible challenge. But Bertholf had only two sets of dogs and two sleds to carry this enormous load. According to Jarvis's orders, he was to be given another team and sled at Unalakleet, but there was none available to him. The best he could do was elicit a promise at the village's trading company that when he reached the settlement of Koyuk, some four days away, another team of dogs and another sled would be waiting for him.

On January 16, with the temperature hovering at nearly forty degrees below zero, Bertholf and his native companion, now accompanied by several additional guides and helpers, set out for Koyuk. Fortunately, his route was across an open landscape that he might have expected would make for much easier traveling. But as he was rapidly learning, in the Arctic winter, there was no such thing. "Our guide," he would later write, "led us through a comparatively level country, and had the snow not been very deep and soft, we would have made a quick trip across. As it was, we were obliged to use snow-shoes nearly all the time, and often had to tramp back and forth ahead of the [dogs] in order to pack the snow down for the little fellows."

By this time, Bertholf, while still hardly a veteran of the frozen North, had learned much about how to cope with the hardships of Arctic winter travel.

As Bertholf would discover, traveling with such heavy loads, even over relatively unchallenging terrain, could present potential problems.

In particular, he had become skilled in meeting the challenge of camping out overnight in the frozen wilderness areas between villages.

"One of us," Bertholf would write, "would pitch the tent while another chopped a supply of firewood, and still another unharnessed the dogs and unloaded the sleds, [making sure that the provisions were securely covered,] for the dogs would devour everything left within reach. Boots or . . . clothing left carelessly exposed were always found half chewed in the morning, for the poor little fellows never get a square meal when travelling in the winter, and are ravenous. We would then start the fire in the stove, and another outside the tent to help melt the snow or ice, to obtain water for drinking and cooking. The beans, which had been boiled before starting, were always frozen so solid they had to be chopped off with the axe, and indeed everything that had the least moisture in it was frozen solid in a day. Our meals consisted of pork and beans cooked in the camp kettle, tea, and, when the hard bread gave out, 'flap-jacks.' We would mix up a batter of flour and water, and make the flap-jacks as large as the frying-pan to save time, using the bacon for grease, and when that was gone seal oil took its place."

Bertholf quickly learned that nothing was more important than caring for the dogs. "After the meal was finished," he would relate, "we would proceed to the very trying task of feeding the dogs. Each man took in his arms one dried fish for each dog, and then tried to get his team all together and away from the others. The poor hungry little fellows would jump up after the fish, and in their eagerness to obtain a mouthful it was a difficult matter to keep from being knocked down and bitten. But finally a fish would be thrown to each one, and then you would have to stand by with a club to drive off any dog that gulped his fish down and then tried to steal from the others. As soon as all the fish intended to be used had been given out and devoured, and the dogs saw no more was coming, they would lie down quietly and go to sleep, and we would then go to our tent [and] close the flap to keep out as much cold air as possible."

On January 20, having spent four days traveling through snowstorms so violent that Bertholf and his party often could see no farther than twenty yards ahead, they reached Koyuk, where supposedly another sled and team of dogs were waiting for them. But they were not there. To make matters much worse, Bertholf's native companion announced that he was homesick and could go no farther. "I was obliged to allow him to return," Bertholf stated, "and was thus left with one dog team with which to transport 1,600 pounds across the country."

It would never do, of course. There was no way that Bertholf could transport that heavy a load with one dog team all the way to Cape Blossom. His only option, he believed, was to head for Golovnin Bay and the reindeer station at Port Clarence, where Jarvis had acquired deer to pull his sleds. Perhaps he could find at least one other dog team and sled there.

Fortunately, Golovnin Bay was nearby. Still, it took all the strength he and his dogs could muster to haul his grossly overloaded sled even the relatively short distance. When he arrived, he was disappointed yet again. There were no dog teams available. But he was told that if he journeyed to where the reindeer herd was located, a few miles away, he would probably be able to acquire deer and deer sleds to help him carry his load. At Golovnin Bay he was also fortunate to encounter a Swedish missionary who was taken with what Bertholf was attempting to accomplish. Concerned that the officer would have great difficulty reaching the reindeer herd with only one dogsled, particularly since there was a mountain that had to be crossed, the missionary loaned Bertholf another sled pulled by two deer, two other dogsleds, and native guides and drivers.

It was an incredibly generous gesture, but Bertholf would quickly discover, as Jarvis earlier had learned, that traveling with both deer sleds and dogsleds was not only a tricky but often a dangerous undertaking. He had been told that the greatest difficulty in traveling with sleds pulled by both deer and dogs was the danger of the dogs following their natural instincts to attack the deer. The solution, he had been informed, was to keep the dogsleds as far behind the deer sled as practical. And from the moment he left Golovnin Bay, he tried to put this advice into practice.

"Having allowed the deer to get good distance ahead, we started," Bertholf would later write, "but my dogs could see the deer, and they started after them at such a speed that the two natives and myself could scarcely keep up

Ellsworth Bertholf's success in bringing the supplies to Cape Blossom was a major achievement—one that, as he was quick to acknowledge, would not have been possible without the hospitality of the indigenous people he encountered along the way.

with them, and we all piled on the sled. The weight of we three, in addition to the heavy load the sled already carried, would have stopped a dog team short under ordinary circumstances, but in their eagerness to overtake the deer the dogs did not apparently mind the extra weight, and bowled along as fast as ever, and before the deer reached the base of the mountain we had to cross, the dogs had caught up with them, and it required the united efforts of the two natives and myself to hold them in check.

"We now held the dogs back until the deer could get far in advance up the mountain, and, as [we had] another sled coming behind with a heavy load, I told one of my natives to wait for it and help the man who was driving it. . . . Owing to my imperfect knowledge of the language, however, the natives misunderstood me, and both of them started back for the rear sled. This released the dogs, and, though I dragged back with all my strength, they started up the mountain side . . . at a pretty good gait, howling and straining in their eagerness to catch the deer, which they imagined would afford them a meal. . . .

"Just as the dogs dashed ahead I saw the two natives start back, and shouted for one of them to come along, but I saw he could not catch us, and the blinding snow soon shut him from my sight. The dogs were now racing up a pretty steep grade, dragging a heavy load along, at a rate I would have thought impossible had I not actually seen it, and, as I did not know the proper trail and there was some danger of getting lost in the blizzard, I put forth every endeavor to overturn the sled, and thus stop the dogs until my native could catch up. I found I was unable to do it, however, and then tried the plan of running ahead and throwing myself down on the head dogs, but the rest of them soon [shook me off], and the whole team would start ahead again.

"Then I thought if I could get under the sled I could raise one side up sufficient to overturn it, so I waited until I had caught my breath, and then ran ahead, threw myself between the dogs, caught hold of the middle [rope], and allowed myself to be dragged along over the snow. This made the dogs slacken their pace, but still did not stop them entirely, so I let myself back toward the sled, still holding on to the [rope], until the whole of my body as far as my shoulders was under the sled between the runners. We were not going very fast now, and suddenly letting go of the [rope], I dug my hands in the snow, and raised my back at the same time. This threw the sled over on one runner, which capsized it and brought the team to a full stop."

It had been an extraordinary experience, one in which Bertholf could have been badly injured—or worse. But the situation was serious enough to warrant his efforts. He had acted heroically in stopping the dogsled and preventing the dogs from catching and devouring the deer. But by now, the deer sled was far up the mountain. And the guides and dogs pulling the other sleds were well behind him. His only option was to wait until they reached him and then, exhausted as they all were, have them make their way over the mountain. For the next two days, men and dogs fought their way up the steep slopes, trying to ignore the relentless wind-driven snow. Finally, they reached the Golovnin Bay reindeer station. And here, at last, Bertholf was rewarded with good fortune, acquiring seven deer and sleds, along with both a Laplander and an Alaskan driver. His luck continued when, just as he was finishing loading up the newly acquired sleds, the snow finally abated. He and his party were able to make it all the way to the Quaker mission house of Reverend Robert Samms, where, as Jarvis had ordered, he was to deliver the supplies.

Tom Lopp pauses while driving the herd toward Cape Blossom as the temperature plunges to forty-five degrees below zero. "It was blowing a gale and the snow was so thick we could not see any distance," he would later write in his log. "Becoming chilled, I put on a fourth parka, making in all two squirrel skin parkas and two reindeer parkas."

CHAPTER NINE

A Hazardous Crossing

Never in his life had David Jarvis experienced such mixed feelings. The relief he felt at having acquired the reindeer was overwhelming, as was his admiration for both Tom Lopp and Charlie Artisarlook. But as powerful as these feelings were, they were tempered by something Lopp had told him as they were about to make their preparations for leaving Cape Prince of Wales.

From the beginning, despite all those who doubted it would be possible, Jarvis had harbored the hope that he would be able to reach the whalers by late May. But Lopp informed him that most of the female deer who made up more than half the herd were pregnant and would be having their calves in late April. Once that took place, the reindeer could not be driven any farther. It was clear—no matter what stood in the way, they would have to get to Point Barrow before the calves were born.

"The journey and task ahead of us was a hazardous one, any way we might look at it, and it was necessary before starting to make the most careful and ample preparations," Jarvis would later write. "We were making an experiment; no such undertaking had ever before been tried in Alaska, and we could not tell how long it would require to travel the 700 miles ahead of us. . . . It was necessary to fit out the party to be independent of villages, from the beginning to the end of the journey. . . . The dogs at any [village] might disperse our deer herd and leave us stranded. We had a great amount of work to accomplish before we could start. Sleds must be built, the herders must be fitted out properly with clothing . . . tents, stoves, camp gear, and spare harness, and lassoes must be made. Clothing was the most important item, for herding and driving are particularly hard on [deerskin] clothes, and everything available was bought and made up, for, even if we did not need it [now], it would be invaluable at Point Barrow."

Jarvis had arrived at Cape Prince of Wales on January 24, 1898, but it took four more days for all of these preparations to be made, and for Lopp's herd, which was grazing some twenty miles from his house, to be rounded up. Meanwhile, Dr. Call and Artisarlook had gone back to Cape Rodney to bring his reindeer to join up with Lopp's. Finally, on the second of February, filled with accounts of the struggles they had had taking the deer across mountains and through storms and deep snow, Call and Artisarlook arrived. "Things had now a much more assuring aspect," a relieved Jarvis would write, "and we were all anxious to get off on what we hoped would be a successful journey, but which had doubtful points about it that could not be foretold."

On February 3, 1898, the now greatly expanded Overland Relief Expedition set out from Cape Prince of Wales, bound first for Cape Blossom and then, at last, for Point Barrow. It was an extraordinary procession. Tom Lopp with three of his herders, all driving light sleds, rode at the back of the herd of 438 reindeer, keeping them moving along. Following them were two "trains" of supply sleds, consisting of four sleds each, and a third train that was made up of five sleds. A single deer was hitched to each supply sled. To make certain that all these sleds moved in unison, they were all tied together. "In this way," Jarvis would write, "one man handled four or five sleds, and many are the tangles and jumbles the animals get into when going up and down the hills, for in trains like this the deer soon worry themselves into a state of excitement."

Aside from Lopp and the herders, there was another important member of the deer-herding contingent, a specially trained "deer dog." "This little fellow," Jarvis explained, "circled around the outer edges of the herd and kept the deer from straying. If one [deer] started from the herd, the dog was after him, barking at his heels until he returned. In this way the deer were kept moving along in one compact body."

But as well organized as the deer drive was, the herd did not move along without interruption. George Fred Tilton had warned that the reindeer would have difficulty finding food. Jarvis could only fret as the animals kept stopping to dig in the snow to get at the moss that lay beneath. But there was nothing he could do to speed up the process.

Even before they had started out, Lopp had convinced Jarvis that because of the near tragedies he had suffered on his previous deer-driving experiences, Jarvis should ride passively in one of the sleds. Call, on the other hand, was convinced that he could do much better than his fellow officer and persuaded Lopp to let him give it a try. The doctor's one brief experiment at the reins quickly provided one of the lighter moments of the entire expedition. "[Dr. Call] furnished much amusement for the boys," Lopp later lightheartedly recounted. "His deer made many circles, some large and some small, turned his sled over a number of times, and gave the Doctor more exercise than he had had for some time."

The ever-serious Jarvis, however, was not amused at what he regarded as yet another delay in their desperate mission. Finally, Jarvis could stand the pace no longer. As they made camp for the evening, he told Lopp that he had decided that once they reached their next destination, the small coastal village of Sinrazat, he and Call would leave the procession and go on ahead.

"We were not essential to the progress of the herd," Jarvis would write, "Mr. Lopp and his herders having all the knowledge and experience necessary for the work in hand, and we . . . were just so much more to be hauled." Aside from meeting up with Bertholf, he had another reason for hastening ahead. To reach Cape Blossom and Reverend Samms's mission, where he hoped the lieutenant would be waiting for him, he would have to cross Kotzebue Sound. His hope was that he would be able to save valuable time by crossing the sound's frozen surface rather than by taking the much longer route around it. But he had been told that, even in the dead of winter, storms could break up the ice in the sound, making it impossible to cross. He simply had to know the condition of the ice, not only for his own sake but also because Lopp would have to decide whether or not to cross the sound with the deer.

What Jarvis already knew was that just getting to Kotzebue Sound was

The villages that Jarvis and his party passed by on their way to Kotzebue Sound were the poorest the lieutenant had encountered on his entire journey. Not only were there no dogs to be had, but there was also no chance of obtaining any food for himself or his hungry companions.

going to be a great challenge. His dogs were bound to become worn out as they hauled the sleds over snow that promised to get even deeper and crustier with each passing mile. The sleds were also likely to take a beating on the rugged terrain. Along the way he would have to find villages where he could purchase new dogs and new sleds, and find people to man the sleds. And he could not even consider making such a trip without the help of a guide who knew the treacherous territory. Luck was with him. On the morning after they all reached Sinrazat, a man named Perninyuk, whom Lopp identified as being one of the best of all native guides, appeared in the expedition's camp, looking for work. Immediately, Jarvis hired him for the journey to Kotzebue Sound.

On February 7, Jarvis, Call, and Perninyuk started out for the small settlement of Toatut on the shore of Kotzebue Sound, fully expecting to be able

The particularly rugged terrain that Jarvis and his companions encountered on their journey to Kotzebue Sound was hard not only on the men and dogs but on the sleds as well. More than once, the trek had to be halted while repairs were made.

to acquire dogs and guides along the way. Almost immediately it became a frustrating experience. "The natives along this part of the coast," Jarvis would recount, "were very poor, and scattered in small numbers at distances of about 20 miles apart. Sealing had been very poor. In some places their dogs had starved, and the people themselves had little to eat. . . . It seemed impossible to get anyone . . . to go along with us more than one day's journey from his own home. The best we could do during the day was about 20 or 25 miles, and at night it was a long, trying ordeal, to buy, borrow, or hire dogs, sleds, and men to go on to the next village.

"Our trials were many and exasperating. We would buy or hire dogs, only to have them run away and return to their owners after going but a short distance with us. . . . Finally, by bribing, threatening, and offering shiploads of provisions, we managed to reach Toatut. . . . We were completely worn out, and our provisions had been drawn upon so extensively . . . that hardly more remained now than a few broken crackers, enough beans for a day, and some tea. . . . Finally, [here at Toatut] all the [natives] except [Perninyuk left] us and [took] their sleds with them, and I think [they did so] mainly because they thought we would starve, for evidently they had no faith in my story of the sled loads of provisions awaiting us at Cape Blossom."

Jarvis could hardly blame them. He was having his own doubts about whether Bertholf would be waiting for him at Reverend Samms's mission. Jarvis wrote, "It was more than 40 miles over the ice to Cape Blossom, where I [hoped] Lieutenant Bertholf was waiting for us with his load of provisions and probably wondering what had become of us, for we were now about a week behind our plans. I was tired and worried. We had been separated since December 20 and had heard absolutely nothing of Bertholf's whereabouts or his progress since that time, and did not know even if he had arrived at St. Michael. I had left him at [Ki-yi-lieug-a-mute] to wait for dogs. Had they come on time or did they have to wait? Had any accident or sickness befallen him and had he been able to [complete his journey] with his heavy load? Was the snow too deep or soft, and had he been stalled somewhere? There were [few] people in all that long route and he had to depend on his preparations [almost] entirely. His provisions we were now greatly in need of, and our progress from here on absolutely depended on them."

"Absolutely depended," indeed. Jarvis was almost totally out of food and still had the long, treacherous sound to cross. Here at Toatuk he had been able to replace some of the men who had deserted him, but almost all of them had made it clear that they would not even consider making the crossing until, after spending the night resting, one of them went out on the sound, walked a considerable distance across it, jumped up and down upon the ice, and determined whether or not it was safe to cross.

When dawn broke the next day, the guide whom his fellows had chosen to test the ice left on his mission, stating that he intended to travel so far out on the sound that it would undoubtedly be dark before he returned. For Jarvis it became yet anther anxious period. "All the next day," he wrote, "we were compelled to wait, idly gazing at the mountains on the other side

The Quaker mission at Cape Blossom stood at the very edge of Kotzebue Sound. For Jarvis and Bertholf, it was a vital destination point.

[of the sound] and wondering whether there was more to eat there than on our side."

Finally, the man who had gone out on the sound to test conditions returned. And, he reported, the ice, as far as he had gone, was good and hard. He and the other natives would accompany Jarvis, Call, and Perninyuk across the sound the next day.

They got underway at eight o'clock the next morning. The ice was indeed solid, but in many places the continual storms had heaved it up into huge mounds. By nightfall they had still not reached the opposite shore, and the men begged Jarvis to stop and make camp for the night on the ice. But he would have none of it. Navigating by the stars and hauling their sleds around the mounds, they finally completed the crossing shortly before midnight. Directly before them stood the village of Kikiktaruk, where the Quaker mission was located.

For the third time on his journey, David Jarvis was approaching a doorway behind which lay an answer that profoundly affected the expedition's chances of saving the whalers. He was closer to Point Barrow than anyone might have hoped for. But time was running out. There was simply no way of going on if Bertholf had not been able to complete his mission. Had he made it? Were the supplies there?

Jarvis and Bertholf pose with residents of the Samms mission and indigenous people of the area. Although great uncertainties still lay ahead for the two men, their reunion was a most welcome relief.

CHAPTER TEN

Dire News of the Whalers

Bertholf was there with the supplies! Later, in his official report, Jarvis would write, "We were relieved and overjoyed. Everything at this end had turned out well, although Lieutenant Bertholf had a hard time. . . . But he arrived all right, with the provisions intact, and we were now fully able to prepare all parts of the expedition for the long and hazardous journey to Point Barrow."

David Jarvis was a man not given to exaggeration. But even for him, saying Bertholf "had hard time" was a colossal understatement. What was not an understatement was Jarvis's prediction that the final three-hundred-mile trip from Cape Blossom to Point Barrow would be a "long and hazardous journey." Adding to his concern was the fact that he had no idea where the herd was at this point. Before crossing Kotzebue Sound, he had left a note for Lopp telling him that it was probably too risky to try to take so many animals across so large an expanse of the always unpredictable ice.

"I paid off and sent back the Laplander and the natives who had come in Lieutenant Bertholf's train, except one native herder, Okitkun, who was retained to care for the deer [Bertholf] brought," Jarvis wrote. "I knew him as a thoroughly good and reliable Eskimo, and, moreover, an excellent deerman — one of the best in the country, and I wanted him here when our herd came along . . . in case any of our herders had [become worn out]."

Aside from his concern over Lopp's whereabouts, Jarvis had something else on his mind. He had heard absolutely nothing about the condition of the whalers at Point Barrow since accidentally encountering George Fred Tilton. Cape Blossom was less than a week's trek away from the trading post and whaling station at Point Hope, and he was certain that someone there would have news of the whalers. It would mean backtracking, but as long as he had to wait for Lopp for at least a week—if not more, depending on his route at Kotzebue Sound—Jarvis felt it was a trip worth taking.

On February 16, after leaving Bertholf behind to rest and wait for Lopp and the deer, Jarvis and Call set out for Point Hope. They were able to move along at a rapid pace, but they could not help noticing that at no time did the temperature rise above thirty-five degrees below zero. It was an awareness that led Jarvis to reflect on the precautions the expedition had taken against the often devastating effects of the bitter cold.

"The difference between care and carelessness is slight, in arctic travel," he would write, "and the first let-up is sure to bring its reminder in the shape of a frosted toe or finger or a frozen nose. One must be on guard, and the slightest tinge in the nose or cheek must be heeded, and circulation started again by vigorous rubbing. . . . I saw a case where the end of a man's nose had dropped off from frostbite. . . . No part of the body requires more attention than [the hands and feet]; socks and boots must be well made and kept thoroughly dry; even the slightest perspiration will, if one stops too long, work disastrously. Both boots and socks should be changed immediately upon going into camp, and dry ones must be put on in the morning before starting. The natives know the importance of this only too well, and if they see one inclined to neglect these precautions, they will insist on his taking care of his foot gear."

On the morning of February 20, Jarvis and Call pulled up at Point Hope's whaling and trading station. Jarvis wrote, "It was reported that a man [named Ned Arey] had just come from Point Barrow. Here was the news I . . . had come all this way to obtain." Immediately, Jarvis began to question Arey, who had a disturbing story to tell. In March 1897, Arey had left San Francisco aboard a whaling vessel, intending to transfer to another ship in the vicinity of Point Barrow. He never met up with the second ship, and a month ago he

had left Point Barrow for Point Hope. He reported that the situation at Point Barrow was growing worse every day. George Fred Tilton had stated that the whalers would run out of food in July. Arey, however, predicted that the food would begin running out in May. One man had already died from freezing. And, Arey added, the dreaded disease scurvy had broken out, particularly among those who had remained aboard the *Belvedere*.

Jarvis reconsidered his plans. Without delay he would send Dr. Call to Point Barrow to let those there know that help was on its way. But the next day, just as Call was about to leave, a messenger suddenly appeared, carrying a long message addressed to Jarvis that made him change his plans again. It was from Lopp, and it contained welcome news. Lopp and his herders had managed to take the deer across the frozen and treacherous Kotzebue Sound. Not, however, as the message revealed, without great difficulty.

Lopp and the herd had arrived at Toatut a few days after Jarvis, Call, and their native helpers had left the village and crossed the sound. Once at Toatut,

The whaling and trading station at Point Hope. Although the photographer (probably Dr. Call) did not identify those in the picture and their heavy clothing obscures their appearances, the group most likely includes Lieutenant Jarvis, Ned Arey, and employees of the whaling and trading station.

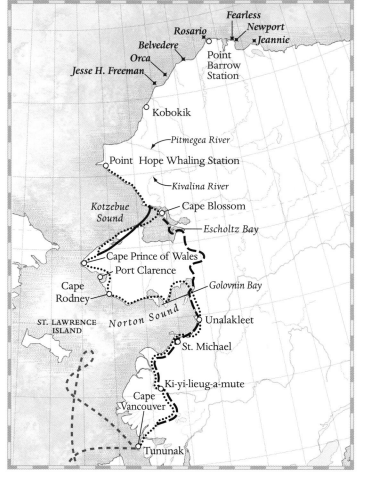

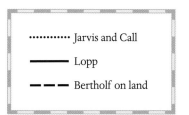

Jarvis and Call

Lopp

Bertholf on land

Lopp had faced making the same decision Jarvis had confronted. Did he dare to travel all the way across the frozen sound, particularly with more than four hundred unpredictable reindeer in tow? Lopp was well aware that to brave the ice meant putting the lives of the herders and their helpers at risk, to say nothing of the deer. Unlike Jarvis, who was prone to making decisions on his own, Lopp put the decision to a vote. To a man, it was agreed that the time that would be saved in crossing the frozen body of water was worth the risk.

It was a decision that almost cost them dearly. After leading the reindeer out onto the sound early in the morning, the party traveled all day and well into the night across the ice, which in some places was so high and so rough that they feared their sleds would be destroyed. Finally, still ten miles from the opposite shore, they had to set up camp. They were so worn out that they neglected to tie the deer to heavy objects to keep them from wandering away, and the exhausted men fell asleep. And paid the price.

The restless and hungry deer wandered off and retraced their steps all the way back to Toatut, where they had last found moss to eat before starting across the sound. When they awoke, the startled herders had no choice but to retrace their steps, round up the deer, and start out over the sound again. This time they were determined not to stop, and by traveling all day and all night made it across. Both the men and the deer, Lopp stated in his message, were "almost dead from hunger and fatigue." Six sled deer had become so exhausted that Lopp had been forced to leave them on the ice. But the crossing had been made, valuable time had been saved, and, as Lopp reported, all would be in good condition again once they had some food and a brief rest.

Lopp's message also informed Jarvis that he and the herd were now camped at the Kivalina River and that while both his men and the deer got the rest they so badly needed, he would wait for Jarvis and Call to join him and the herd. Jarvis and Call hastened out of Point Hope and soon came upon the river. That night, however, it began to snow so hard that they were forced to halt and seek refuge in a small native hut. When they awoke early the next morning, the snow had turned into a blizzard so fierce that, despite Jarvis's frustration, they were trapped inside the hut until the storm finally abated the next day. Now winding their way along the Kivalina, they were suddenly halted by an excited young boy from the area who came running up, shouting that he had seen a huge herd of reindeer. Immediately, Jarvis sent his guide off with the boy to find Lopp and bring him to where he and Call were waiting. Lopp arrived, looking much the worse for wear. Lopp, Jarvis would recall, "showed the marks of frozen cheeks and nose that all his party had gotten in their hard trip over the ice of Kotzebue Sound."

With more than four hundred reindeer and supplies roughly in the same place, Jarvis continued, they "had fully 400 miles more of travel against the northeast wind that generally prevails in this part of the country during the

Replacing the dogs with fresh animals was both a necessity and a constant challenge. Here, Dr. Call looks over a new team he has acquired at Point Hope.

winter, and only [the] month of March to do it in." With that in mind, Jarvis decided that Lopp and the herd should start out for the mountains as soon as possible. Jarvis and Call would return to Point Hope to gather up the supplies they had left behind in their haste to find Lopp at the Kivalina River. They would then rejoin Lopp and the herd once they crossed the mountains.

Before setting off to rejoin the herd, Jarvis made another decision as well. His conversation with Ned Arey had troubled him more than he let on to either Dr. Call or Tom Lopp. The more he thought about it, the more he became deeply concerned that if, as Arey had predicted, the provisions at Point Barrow ran out in May, things there would be truly desperate by the time he hopefully arrived. Once again he made a change in plans, and once again it involved Lieutenant Bertholf.

Just as he was about to catch up with Lopp, Jarvis sent a guide back to the Quaker mission with a message for the lieutenant. In it, Jarvis informed Bertholf that if, upon reaching Point Barrow, he found the situation to be disastrous, he was going to send at least one hundred of the whalers to be cared for at Point Hope. Bertholf, Jarvis ordered, was to leave immediately for Point Hope to prepare for the arrival of the whalemen if Jarvis found such a move necessary.

On March 6, 1898, Jarvis and Call were ready to start out again to find the herd. But even the seemingly tireless Jarvis had to admit that the journey thus far in general, and the trips back and forth to Point Hope in particular, had taken their toll. In what was for him a rare admission, he wrote, "We had now come so great a distance that, while we were somewhat hardened to the work, we had been at it so long we were necessarily tired, and could not stand running ahead of the dogs all the time as had to be done in this part of the country. . . . I finally engaged a middle-aged man and wife, who had lived at Point Barrow several years. They had never been over the road we were to travel, but we could follow the coast and I wanted them more to help with the sleds than for any particular guidance. Nekowrah, the man, while not a good traveler, was the best man around a camp I ever saw, and his judgment and foresight in these matters saved us much discomfort, if not suffering. It is characteristic of the natives of the extreme north that they have an excellent knowledge of how to prepare for and withstand the rigors of the climate. They seem to have no fears of it, but at the same time are fully alive to its dangers and menaces."

As they traveled, Jarvis could not shake his concerns. He worried about whether Lopp could steer the herd over the rugged mountains. And he was worried about what he and Call would encounter as well. "We had been warned concerning the blizzards on this coast," Jarvis would write, "and I had heard many stories of the terrible times of parties who had been caught in these storms. One party I knew of had been storm-bound for forty-two days . . . and were compelled to eat their dogs before the storm passed over. We had never allowed the darker side of the stories we had heard to trouble us, except so far as to make our preparations more complete, yet often during our long flight up this coast if one had dared let down we might have been left somewhere on the road."

By this time, Jarvis and Call had become expert at coping with the conditions. "We had now been traveling so long that our camping and packing sleds had been reduced to a system," Jarvis wrote. "There were four of us and each had his own part of the work to do. The doctor was the cook and looked out for the stove and the food. I attended to the sleds and the tent. The native woman [Shucungunga] was the doctor's assistant and besides looked after our clothes, while her husband Nekowrah helped me and did the heavy work. On coming to our camping place, Nekowrah and I would get out the tent and pitch it. This done, the doctor would set up his stove, while Nekowrah went on a hunt for wood, and I would bank up the snow around the sides to keep the wind out and secure the hut generally. Then the sleds were unpacked and all our sleeping gear, food, and cooking utensils were passed in to Shucungunga, who arranged them inside. By this time the fire was started in the stove, the dogs were unharnessed, and the sleds put beyond their reach. This would all take from one-half to three-quarters of an hour, and in that time the tent would be good and warm and we could go inside and change our clothes. The wet ones were passed over to Shucungunga for drying, who stretched a line along the ridgepole and hung up the clothes to catch all the warm air possible."

On March 10, Jarvis and Call reached the mouth of the Pitmegea River, where they were supposed to meet Lopp and the reindeer. "[I] looked anxiously around for some sign of the deer herd," Jarvis wrote, "and saw sticking in the snow a cross made of two pieces of bread box, [with a sign upon it.]" Once he got close enough to the sign, Jarvis saw that it read, "Letter between boards." Then, after tearing the boards apart, he found a note addressed to him. It was from Lopp, and it was just what Jarvis wanted to hear. After spending six grueling days crossing the mountains, Lopp and the herd had arrived at this spot on March 7. The sled deer were nearly "played out," but the herd was in as good shape as could be expected. He and his fellow herders, Lopp concluded, had taken a one-day rest and then, on the ninth, had started out again for Point Barrow.

Jarvis was overjoyed. Not only had the mountains been crossed, and seemingly without the loss of a single deer, but for the first time since the long trek with the reindeer had started, the deer were actually ahead of him.

Anxious to catch up with Lopp, Jarvis pushed through the steady cold and relentless northeast wind. "We were wet through with perspiration," he would write, "and had to [keep] moving until we camped at night to keep from freezing for it is almost fatal to stop with wet clothes."

Incredibly, the weather got even worse. On March 15, the snow began to come down so hard that Jarvis's group could not see ahead more than a few feet. At the same time, the temperature dropped to more than forty degrees below zero, the coldest Jarvis had yet encountered. He had no choice but to halt his pursuit of the herd and set up camp. "It was all we could do," he would write, "to keep the tent from blowing down, so we cut blocks of snow and built a barricade around our camp that kept off some of the wind, but still it was anything but comfortable, and as the old native hut [that was nearby] was filled with hard, packed snow and we could not get in there . . . we had to finally tear off its covering of wood to get enough to keep our fires going."

They were uncomfortable, but they were safe. What Jarvis could not abide, however, was that for two more days and nights the conditions refused to improve. Finally, on the morning of the seventeenth, the storm abated.

Leaving the tent at last, Jarvis found his dogs buried in drifts so high that only their noses stuck out. Before they could move on, an agonizing amount of time had to be spent uncovering buried equipment, including the sleds, and removing mounds of snow from the tent before it could be packed away.

Pushing on, they reached a settlement of only two huts, where they learned that Lopp and the deer had passed through only a short time before. They picked up the pace as best they could, and soon, as Jarvis would write, "we could see [the herd] ahead, like a small black cloud sweeping over the sea of intense white snow." The snow kept falling so hard that even with Lopp so agonizingly close, Jarvis had to make camp for the night. Lying in his tent, he decided that, in order to make the fastest time possible, the next day he would lighten his sled, leave Call and the rest of his party behind in the camp, and pursue Lopp and the herd alone. It was a decision totally out of character for the normally cautious Jarvis. He well knew the dangers involved in traveling alone in the Arctic in the dead of winter. With no one around to help him, one bone-breaking spill over a hidden boulder, one plunge through the ice into a snow-covered stream, or any one of countless other dire accidents in subzero temperatures could prove fatal. But he had to catch up with the herd. He had to get to Point Barrow.

With the snow still pounding down, it took him another full day and night to find the herd. When he caught up with the group, he was relieved to find Lopp and the reindeer in good condition. As Lopp had indicated in his note, the deer that had been pulling the sleds were exhausted. And all across the mountains, the deep snow had made it extremely difficult for the animals to get at the moss that lay beneath. After assuring himself that the herd was all right, Jarvis decided that he could now go back to camp, where he had left Call and the guides, so that they could all hasten on to Point Barrow and the whalers.

Throughout their separate journeys to Cape Blossom, Lopp and Jarvis periodically left messages for each other indicating their whereabouts. Here, Jarvis finds a note from Lopp.

The construction of snow houses required the efforts of several individuals. Primitive as they appeared, the houses were remarkably warm even during the coldest winter months.

CHAPTER ELEVEN

Contact

The week that followed was truly remarkable. Traveling separately, Lopp and the deer and Jarvis and his party were daily battered with blizzards. Throughout this entire time, although the two groups were relatively near each other, each had no idea where the other was because of the blinding snow. On one occasion, Lopp and the entire herd passed within a half mile of Jarvis and his companions without either group knowing of the other.

What they had seen as they tried to keep moving in the horrendous conditions were several structures that the indigenous people built when forced to set up camp. "The favorite way among the Eskimos of camping in this part of the country," Jarvis explained, "is to build snow houses. . . . The wind packs the snow so hard that with a long knife it can be cut into blocks like building stone, and in a short time a small strong house can be constructed with these, the chinks being stopped up with loose snow, and a large block used as a door to close the opening, making the place nearly airtight. Soon the warmth of the bodies of three or four people, together with the heat from a native seal-oil lamp or kerosene-oil stove, will raise the temperature of the place so that it is fairly comfortable, and one can even remove some of his clothing. On account of the difficulties of construction, a snow house can not be so large as a tent, and the oil for the stove adds greatly to the weight to be carried; but, when traveling back from the coast, where there is no wood, snow houses are the necessity of

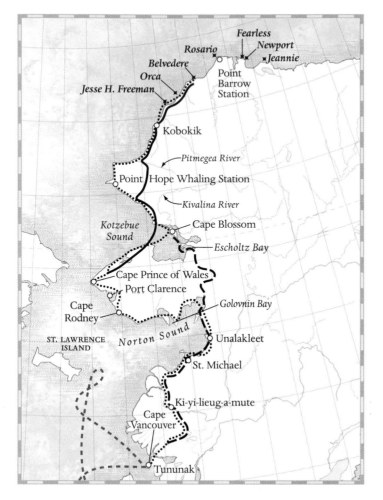

.... Jarvis and Call

———— Lopp

— — — Bertholf on land

– – – – The *Bear*'s winter route

circumstances. As such they are made the best of, and whatever discomforts they entail are passed off as unavoidable and not thought of."

By the afternoon of March 25, Lopp had to pause to allow the deer to forage for food. Jarvis and Call managed to put a good deal of distance between themselves and the herd. Suddenly, off in the distance, Jarvis spotted objects rising high out of the ice and snow. Even from afar, they looked to him like masts, rigging, and a smokestack. But could he trust what he was seeing? Earlier in his trek across Cape Blossom, he had noted that, because of the Arctic light and the unique nature of the vast terrain, "almost every twig or stick that stuck up through the snow stood out against the extreme whiteness of the surrounding country and seemed exaggerated into the size of a telegraph pole at least. . . . Every little ridge or unevenness in the snow seems at first a hill or mountain in your path, and it is not until you get very close to the rise that you are finally convinced of your error."

But this time Jarvis's eyes were not deceiving him. The objects in the distance really were a mast, rigging, and a smokestack. One hundred and three days after landing at least 1,500 miles away, Jarvis and Dr. Call had spotted one of the icebound whaling vessels, the *Belvedere*. "We drew up alongside about 4 p.m.," Jarvis would later write, "and going aboard announced ourselves and our mission, but it was some time before the first astonishment and incredulousness could wear off and a welcome be extended to us."

Thrilled as he was to have reached the first of the stricken ships, Jarvis was alarmed at what he discovered aboard the *Belvedere*. "Captain Millard," he would report, "was a very sick man and looked as if he would hardly survive the winter. There were 30 men on board the vessel at that time, 15 of her crew having been sent to Point Barrow. . . . Provisions were very short. . . . They were wholly dependent upon hunting for meat . . . but the hunting season was drawing to a close. . . . In November last a Siberian Eskimo, one of the crew of the *Orca,* had wandered off to go to his home in Siberia and was never heard of again. A man named Kelly, water tender of the *Orca,* who had been retained on board the *Belvedere* because he was not able to travel to Point Barrow, was a pitiable object from [illness]. He applied to Surgeon Call for treatment, but was beyond help, and a few days after we left, his body was found in the stern hole, where it was thought he had jumped to end his misery."

As dire as the situation was aboard the *Belvedere,* Jarvis and Call knew there was little they could do until the herd arrived and they assessed the situation at Point Barrow. The next day they left the vessel and headed for Barrow itself. It was now March 28, and they were embarking on the very last leg of their long ordeal. But, as if to accentuate all they had gone through, they were halted by yet another raging blizzard and had to set up camp. But this time, Jarvis was not frustrated by the delay. Instead, he spent the evening in his tent reflecting upon the entire adventure.

To Jarvis, the ghostly, icebound
Belvedere *was a welcome sight.*

"We were so near our journey's end now," he would write, "that we could afford to look back with a measure of satisfaction. On starting out it was hardly thought or contemplated that we could reach Point Barrow before April, and . . . there were many times, when, considering the difficulties and dangers, I had misgivings as to our being able to arrive within the limited time. Following the windings of the coast . . . we had traveled somewhere in the neighborhood of 1,500 miles or more. We had lived on the country, as we were directed, and had drawn from it all our means of travel, except a part of our camp gear and the small store we brought from the ship. The movements of the reindeer herd had far exceeded

It seemed ages ago that Jarvis and Call had left Tunanuk for Point Barrow, never knowing if they would reach their destination. Now, on March 28, 1898, only one day's journey from the point and the whalers, they were forced by yet another blizzard to set up camp one final time and wait out the storm.

our expectations. . . . Loss of life or serious accident, which were always imminent, had been averted by extreme care, and we were now within 15 miles of our destination."

They awoke in the morning to crisp and clear weather. With great anticipation, finding it difficult to believe that they were only hours from completing their journey, they hurried on. And suddenly, there before them was the settlement at Point Barrow.

"Passing rapidly by the village," Jarvis would recall, "we drew up at the house of the Cape Smythe Whaling and Trading Company, of which Mr. C. D. Brower was manager. . . . When we greeted Mr. Brower and some of the officers of the wrecked vessels, whom we knew, they were stunned, and it

was some time before they could realize that we were flesh and blood. Some looked off to the south to see if there was not a ship in sight, and others wanted to know if we had come up in a balloon. Though they had realized their dangerous situation last fall and had sent out Mr. Tilton . . . for aid . . . they had not thought it possible for anyone to reach them in the winter, and had not we and our positions been so well known, I think that they would have doubted that we really did come in from the outside world."

Startled inhabitants look on as Jarvis and Call pass by their village on their way to Charlie Brower's whaling station. As he would later write, Brower was stunned "when Lieutenant Jarvis and Dr. Call of the cutter Bear came mushing up the coast. My first thought was that they had been wrecked and were coming for aid. As a matter of fact, it was the other way around. They were there to help us."

One of Lieutenant Jarvis's greatest tasks once he reached Point Barrow was to keep the men aboard the still stranded ships supplied with food and other provisions. Here, one of the supply parties makes its way toward the vessels.

CHAPTER TWELVE

Jarvis Takes Charge

They had made it! And, it seemed, they had made it on time. A day after their arrival, Lopp and the herd arrived as well. "When the herd arrived in good condition and a good and sufficient supply of food was assured, it was a great relief," Jarvis would write. "In coming from Cape Prince of Wales the deer had traveled over 700 miles in fifty-five days, counting all the delays from storms and preparations, and Artisarlook's herd had come 100 miles farther, from Point Rodney. We were all grateful to Mr. Lopp and the 'boys' for what they had done, and I can not speak too highly of the skill, courage, and persistent, untiring work they showed from the beginning to the end of that long journey." It was an extraordinary accomplishment for them all. But what Jarvis and Call would quickly discover was that defying all odds and getting to the whalemen was one thing; keeping them alive until the *Bear* could get to Point Barrow and bring them home was quite another.

Almost as soon as Jarvis and Call made their dramatic appearance at Barrow, they were met by a group of the stranded whalers who had urged them to inspect the bunkhouse and witness the terrible conditions under which they and their fellow sailors had been living. Then they pleaded with the officers to do whatever they could to improve these conditions.

The two officers wasted no time in making their inspection and were shocked by what they encountered. It was an even more serious situation than

Jarvis had feared. "[The whalemen] were much debilitated and run down," he wrote, "and if something was not done quickly the weaker ones would soon die for general debility, and serious sickness attack all. . . . I determined that changes must be made at once, the men moved from their present quarters, their clothes and bodies cleaned, and proper rules of discipline, health, and exercise enforced."

There was no question in Jarvis's mind that his first priority had to be that of getting the men out of the squalid bunkhouse and into cleaner, healthier quarters. He was determined also to create additional space so that the whalers would not be crammed in so close together.

He began by convincing Dr. Richmond Marsh, a minister and physician who had taken over the Presbyterian mission at Barrow at about the same time the whalers had become stranded, to make the mission's large schoolroom available for some of the whalers to live in. Then he persuaded Ned

Finding enough wood to improve the whalers' living quarters was as great a challenge as feeding the men. Here, wood salvaged from an ancient shipwreck is being hauled to where it can be put to use.

By convincing those who ran the Presbyterian mission at Point Barrow to take in a number of the whalemen, Jarvis accomplished much in the way of improving both the comfort and the health of those he had been sent to rescue.

McIlhenny to share the refuge building with an additional number of whale-men. As Jarvis later explained, "These quarters were all light, dry, and warm, and could easily be inspected." Finally, Jarvis had Brower's men search for whatever scrap lumber they could find and then had them use the lumber to convert one of Brower's warehouses into additional living space. When all this was completed, Jarvis distributed the whalemen throughout the new quarters and had the filthy bunkhouse torn down, saving the wood to be used as fuel for heating and cooking.

For Jarvis, providing healthier and more comfortable quarters for those he had come to rescue was just the first step. So much more needed to be done if the whalers were to survive until the *Bear* came. Thanks to Brower, who had sent a group of villagers out on hunting parties during the two months after the whalers had been shipwrecked, enough ducks, geese, and wild deer had been killed to provide the whalemen with life-sustaining, albeit scanty, rations. But as Brower had anticipated, once the winter set in, hunting had become increasingly difficult.

"Provisions were short, very short," Jarvis had observed on his arrival, "and only by the strictest economy . . . had they been enabled to get along so far." Now, thanks to the deer the expedition had delivered, he was able to order an increase in the whalemen's rations of fresh meat to 2½ pounds per week. And he took another morale-boosting step as well. "I found that the greatest craving of the men was for some seasoning in their food," he wrote. "After my arrival I collected from the outlying vessels some tins of sage, savory, and thyme, and these seemed to make a great difference in the food. Pepper was most craved, but . . . there was little or none . . . anywhere."

The increase that Jarvis made in the whalers' meat ration was important for a reason other than morale. When the opportunities to hunt for fresh meat had diminished dramatically in the winter, the instances of scurvy had increased at an alarming rate. Fortunately, Dr. Call was experienced in dealing with the disease. Within a relatively short period of time, the infusion of fresh deer meat into the whalemen's diet brought an end to the serious threat to so many of their lives. As James Allen would later state, "No one can tell what might have happened had Dr. Call not come just at the right time."

Allen's appreciation of the doctor would come to be shared by all those at Point Barrow. From the moment he arrived, Call would spend most of every day tending not only to the needs of the whalemen quartered there but also to those of some two hundred indigenous families who lived in the area. And his activities would not be confined to Barrow. "At 12:45 p.m. I left . . . on a sick call to the vessels in the ice 100 miles to the eastward," one of the entries in his journal would read. "There were three sleds, two of which were loaded with deer meat, and the third, to which I was assigned, carried food for the dogs. . . . The weather had been mild and the snow was soft and slushy, and for many miles we were compelled to make our way over [large mounds] of ice and to wade through depressions filled with water. We finally reached the first vessel on the third day, [where I treated men suffering from nasal infection, dysentery, and influenza]."

The tireless Samuel Call would make contributions beyond his medical training. As a photographer, he created a unique visual record of the long trek to Point Barrow as well as of the time he spent there. Call would also prove to be a keen observer of the native population's ways of life. Later, he would write about his observations, providing fascinating insights into a unique people whose customs and traditions were so different from his own.

With the issues of housing and illness having been quickly addressed, Jarvis then turned his attention to another of the whalemen's needs. A majority of the men were not adequately clothed for the winter Arctic weather. "Since most of the men still lacked adequate clothing," Charlie Brower would write, "Jarvis now suggested that the Eskimos [who lived in the village at Point Barrow] might be persuaded to [donate the needed garments], each native throwing in whatever clothing he could spare. I didn't know how the Eskimos would take to the idea of helping white men who had stooped so low as to rob their graveyard. But I did my best—and was fairly overwhelmed by their generous response. . . . I was careful to take down the names of all donors, however, and [eventually I] saw that each native was well rewarded. They never forgot that."

From the moment he had arrived at Point Barrow, Jarvis had been appalled at the whalemen's filthy condition. Making it clear to all the whalers that "cleanliness was an absolute necessity," he issued to every man one pound of soap each month and saw to it that enough snow was melted on the stove each day to provide at least a minimum amount of water for the men to clean

Dr. Call pauses on one of his many trips to the men on the stranded ships. Call's medical skills and devotion to duty would be responsible for saving the lives of a great many of the whalemen.

themselves with. With the help of Dr. Call, he then enforced a strict policy of cleanliness and sanitation. "It was difficult at first," Jarvis would recall, "to get some of the men to make any effort to clean themselves; but later, after the majority saw they had the means to do it, and could, they united to compel the others and were quick to report any great neglect. It was not long before the general appearance of all was greatly improved."

Thanks to Jarvis's determination and efforts, the whalers had been removed from their squalid quarters and had been provided with far better living conditions. They had received more adequate clothing. And they had been convinced of the importance of keeping themselves clean. But from Jarvis's first inspection, he knew that with the captains' abdication of responsibility for their men, lack of discipline threatened everything else he could do to keep the whalemen alive.

Less than twenty-four hours after completing his first inspection, Jarvis made it emphatically known that, as the government-appointed authority while the whalers were at Point Barrow, he was assuming total command. As such, he stated, he would set strict rules of behavior and would dictate punishment if they were not followed. He also let everyone know that he and he alone would settle all disputes that arose among the men. "Discipline and obedience came first with Jarvis," James Allen would write, "and we all knew that."

A number of the men began to argue that since their term of employment aboard their ships had expired during their long months imprisoned in the ice, their officers no longer had any authority over them and no longer had to be obeyed. Many of them stated that they now wanted to leave their vessels and join those who were quartered at Point Barrow. After listening to the men's arguments, Jarvis pointed out that those aboard the vessels were serving longer than they

This report, submitted by Dr. Call, lists the medical supplies he carried with him at all times both during the trek to Point Barrow and while treating the whalemen there.

REPORT OF SURG. S. J. CALL, R. C. S.

SEPTEMBER 1, 1898.

SIR: In accordance with your instructions, I have the honor to submit the following medical report of the Overland Relief Expedition during the eight months of travel and isolation from the time we were put upon the beach at Cape Vancouver, December 16, 1897, until the U. S. Revenue Cutter *Bear* arrived and returned with us August 16, 1898.

Knowing from past experience in the Arctic that all whaling vessels, before leaving San Francisco, were furnished with a medical chest containing most of the ordinary medical and surgical supplies, I did not deem it necessary to take more medicines than were needed for our own immediate use and that of any special case met with on the tramp. My outfit, therefore, consisted of a small leather grip containing, besides a few general remedies in tablet form, the following:

1 pocket surgical case.
1 hypodermic case.
1 stethoscope.
¼ pound lint.
1 roll rubber adhesive plaster, 1 inch.
1 fever thermometer.

1 dozen assorted surgical bandages.
½ roll isinglass plaster.
½ dozen surgical sponges.
½ dozen pair snow glasses.
½ dozen toothbrushes.

On account of the prospective low temperature the liquid preparations were reduced to a minimum, and were, 8 ounces A. C. E. mixture, 4 ounces tincture chloride of iron, 4 ounces Friar balsam, and one-third dozen extract ginger.

The medicine grip was an object of considerable care, and was always given the warmest and most protected part of the sled, tent, By taking this precaution none of the liquid medicines

had contracted for entirely because of an act of nature and that, by law, they were still under the command of their captains and other officers.

"Aside from . . . safety . . . there were other strong reasons why the men should remain as they were on their vessels," Jarvis would explain. "All the food had been distributed with this in view, and it was impossible now to make any change in it. I could not care for any more at Point Barrow without cutting down an already too short allowance. Again, in the matter of exercising discipline and control, it was better that the men be divided into small groups, separated at good distances, as they now were, for so many idle men in one crowd would breed all manner of disturbances and troubles."

Preventing the men from leaving their ships was a continuous issue for

Charlie Brower (center) at Point Barrow after the Overland Relief Expedition arrived. "But for [Brower's] care and management," Ellsworth Bertholf would write, "it is certain that many of the men would have perished before the expedition came to their relief."

Jarvis. "Louis Rich, carpenter of the *Fearless*," Jarvis wrote, "arrived at [Point Barrow], reporting he had left his vessel on account of a dispute with the [captain], and asked that he be taken into the quarters with the shipwrecked men. Upon investigation, his cause for leaving was found to be so trivial that I returned him to the vessel the next day and admonished him to remain there. I suspected and subsequently learned that this man was put forward to try me . . . and if he had been allowed to leave the vessel all the other dissatisfied ones would soon have followed. As he had to walk 50 miles coming to me and 50 miles [more] returning to the vessel, there were none others anxious to try it after that lesson."

Addressing all the issues he had encountered ashore at Point Barrow was an awesome task. "After getting the camp in satisfactory order," he stated, "I turned my attention to the outlying vessels. . . . I started [out] with Captain Leavitt, of the *Newport*, to visit his vessel and the others to the east of Point Barrow," Jarvis wrote. "We went by the *Rosario*, and I authorized Captain Coffin to issue fresh meat to his men to the extent of 1½ pounds per day. . . . The steamers *Newport* and *Fearless* were fully 50 miles from [shore], and it was a long day's journey to reach them without camping, yet it was [being] done day after day by the [ships' crews]. . . . After remaining on the *Newport* two days I went on to the *Jeanie* [sic] with Captain Mason, of that vessel, who had been visiting the *Newport*. It was a long journey of 40 to 45 miles over the ice of Smiths Bay, and it was well into the night before we arrived at the vessel."

As Jarvis reflected on his own difficult trips to the vessels and the constant parade of sleds from shore to ships and back again, he became aware once again of the unique animals upon whom he and the others had relied from the beginning of the rescue mission—the sled dogs. "This . . . hauling was very severe on the dogs, as the honeycombed ice lacerated their feet in a short time, and even the boots that were made for their feet saved them very little [pain. The dogs] worked wonderfully, though, and many would arrive back in such a state they could hardly stand up. I know no more faithful, enduring, hard-working animal than an Eskimo dog. There is no snow too deep, no ice too rough, no hill too steep for them to face, and as long as there is life left in them they will pull and struggle to drag along. Ill fed and abused, they may

seem snarling and snappish, but their faithfulness dwarfs all other consider-ations. For my own team, which traveled with different parts of the expedi-tion more than two thousand five hundred miles during the winter, I have only an affectionate gratitude for the way they carried us through. The work of the dogs and [men] from the ships and station and villages about Point Barrow during the long winter was heroic, and . . . grand beyond description."

By the time his first full month at Point Barrow was over, David Jarvis was confident that he had dealt successfully with every crisis he confronted. But there was still one thing in particular that was troubling him. Despite all he had done, he had not managed to find out a single thing about the *Wanderer,* the one ship in the whaling fleet that was still unaccounted for. Had she sunk, taking her officers and crew down with her? Had she become locked in the ice somewhere well out of sight? Neither Jarvis nor anyone else at Point Barrow had a clue.

And then something that no one could possibly have foreseen took place. Just as Jarvis was about to organize a search for the missing ship, a large, sail-bearing sled appeared practically at his doorstep. Among those aboard it was a man who identified himself as being a boat steerer from the whaleship *Mary D. Hume,* which was wintering off Herschel Island. He and his companions, he stated, under orders from their captain, had left their vessel on February 25 to inform the captains of the other ships in the whaling fleet about the condition of their fellow whaleship the *Wanderer.* As Jarvis would later write, "They had a very severe [two-month] trip along an almost deserted coast and at times were compelled to go inland from the coast to hunt for food for themselves and [their] dogs, and when they arrived . . . were in very bad straits."

But they were not in such bad condition that they could not relate the news that they had been sent to deliver. The *Wanderer,* they reported, was

The constant traveling back and forth to the ships still trapped offshore challenged the dogs' stamina. Feeding the animals was an important daily ritual.

safely wintering off Herschel Island. Moreover, its officers and crew were being adequately provided for, thanks to the ample provisions aboard the *Mary D. Hume.*

For Jarvis, "the arrival of this sled removed the last doubtful point in the situation [at Point Barrow]." What remained, he would write, was "simply a question of making the best uses of what we had, and to hold everybody together in order and discipline until [the *Bear's*] arrival." That, of course, was not as simple as Jarvis stated. And he knew it. Holding the men together meant not only maintaining order and discipline but also keeping the men's morale up by finding things for them to do.

In order to accomplish this, Jarvis made daily exercise mandatory for every one of the whalers ashore. He had a duck-shooting camp erected

After a long and arduous journey, the men who carried the news of the Wanderer's whereabouts arrived at Point Barrow.

several miles from where the men were quartered. To his surprise, the activity became so popular that during one ten-day period, the whalemen-turned-hunters killed 1,100 ducks, which also added to the whalers' food supply. Jarvis's main purpose in establishing the far-off camp, however, was to force the men to walk to and from its site. And for those men who, after battling whales, found duck hunting a bore or had an aversion to shooting ducks, he instituted a mandatory activity that required them to walk the distance to the camp and hike back carrying at least ten of the ducks that had been shot.

Gradually, almost all of the men, who had been so idle before Jarvis arrived, came to truly enjoy the exercises he initiated, the shooting or the long walks. But the most popular activity, by far, was baseball. James Allen would later write, "He gave the orders that all those who could play baseball give him their names. Those who did not play baseball [he ordered] must witness the games or take walks.

"Two baseball teams were chosen. McIlhenny was a captain of one side; I was captain of the other," recalled Allen. "Chief Engineer Denny was chosen umpire. He was a former professional baseball player and really knew the game. He accepted under protest; it was either be umpire or carry 10 eider ducks . . . from the ducking station 10 miles away."

For those who played in the games as well as those who watched them, it was a unique experience. As Lieutenant Bertholf would later comment, "A Ball-game with the ground covered with snow and the thermometer away below zero was certainly a novelty."

What was not a novelty, however, was the weeks of waiting for the ice offshore to melt. Even when June arrived, there was not a significant amount of open water to be seen. When the calendar turned to July, the whaleships were still icebound, and amazingly they were still in danger.

"There was nothing left but to wait patiently for the break-up," Jarvis would later write. "Before it came, however, on July 2, we had a violent southeast gale . . . shoving [the ice] farther in, and sending [it] . . . against the beach. One of these crushes struck the stern of the . . . *Rosario* . . . and raised her up on the ice above the level of the water. Passing under her, [the ice] took away her rudder and sternpost, tore her keel away, and stove a hole in her bow. All

this happened in a few minutes, but as the vessel was close up to the beach the crew got ashore safely."

The Rosario *lies crushed after the July 2nd storm.*

Thankfully, there had been no loss of life. But the *Rosario,* which had managed to survive being locked in the ice for more than ten months, had been destroyed. And Lieutenant David Jarvis now had another crew of whalemen to care for at Point Barrow.

The Bear *steams toward Point Barrow. Even so hardened an Arctic veteran as Captain Francis Tuttle could not believe the amount of ice that remained in the region that late into the summer.*

CHAPTER THIRTEEN

Voyage Against Time

In all the years that Point Barrow had been inhabited, no one had ever witnessed anything quite like the July storm that had destroyed the *Rosario*. The *Rosario* was not the only ship to be affected by the storm. At the height of the gale, the enormous ice pack in which the *Belvedere* had long been trapped was torn away from the rest of the ice with the ship still embedded in it. It seemed certain that both the ice pack and the ship would be carried to an uncertain future far out to sea. But then the winds shifted suddenly, and to the amazement of its crew, the *Belvedere* was carried back to almost the exact position it had been in before the storm began — locked in the ice.

Like the *Belvedere,* the *Jeannie* remained stuck fast to the ice field around her. But then the entire mass of ice was shoved violently against the beach, where it came to rest atop other ice that, in places, was as high as forty feet. Throughout the storm, the *Newport* and the *Fearless* remained exactly where they were but were battered so heavily by wind and ice that those aboard could hardly believe that they had not been crushed like the *Rosario*.

Captain Francis Tuttle had no way of knowing about the July 2nd storm that had caused so much havoc at Point Barrow. Two weeks earlier, on June 14, he had steamed the *Bear* out of its winter quarters far to the south at Dutch Harbor, hoping that by now the ice all the way up the coast must have either melted or been blown sufficiently away. He was on his way to Point Barrow to complete his role in the rescue mission that had been launched so many months ago. Tuttle also had no way of knowing if Jarvis, Call, and Bertholf had been able to successfully carry out their unprecedented journey.

On June 19, as he was making his way toward St. Lawrence Bay, he encountered ice so heavy that it took him almost four days to get through it. When he finally reached the bay, he spotted another vessel anchored there. It was the whaleship *William Bayless,* and its captain had news to impart. He told Tuttle that he had encountered Tom Lopp, who reported that he was making his way home to Cape Prince of Wales after having taken a herd of reindeer to Point Barrow. These were all the details that the captain could give him, but to Tuttle, they were exciting enough. Obviously, Jarvis had been able to persuade Lopp to join the expedition. And according to the *Bayless's* captain, Lopp and his reindeer had made it to Point Barrow.

On June 24, the *Bear* reached Cape Prince of Wales, where Tuttle immediately sought out Tom Lopp. Never had he listened to another man's story so intently or anxiously as he did to the reindeer expert's account. The good news, Lopp related, was that Jarvis and Dr. Call had made it all the way to Point Barrow. So, too, he added, had Artisarlook and his reindeer. Bertholf had also performed heroically in carrying out a long, difficult journey to keep the expedition supplied. But, Lopp continued, there was other news as well. Lopp then gave Tuttle a full account of the dire situation at Point Barrow when Jarvis and Call arrived. He concluded by stating that when, on April 14, Jarvis had discharged him so that he might return to his family, the two Cutter Service officers were just beginning the formidable task of trying to improve conditions among the whalers so that they might survive until Tuttle and the *Bear* could get to them.

Having heard Lopp's dramatic account, Tuttle was more aware than ever of the need to get to Point Barrow as quickly as possible. But during his report, Lopp had told him that among the most serious needs the stranded whalemen had was warm clothing. So, after bidding farewell to Lopp, Tuttle immediately doubled back to St. Michael, where he laid in a generous supply of clothes.

Leaving St. Michael and heading north again, Tuttle reached Point Hope on July 15. And there he received yet another surprise. Waiting to greet him was none other than Lieutenant Bertholf. Reacting to the astonished look on Tuttle's face, Bertholf told him that Jarvis had sent him to Point Hope on a special mission. He was to make arrangements for the whaling and trading station there to take in some of the stranded whalers in case the *Bear* did not arrive at Point Barrow by the middle of August. With this done, he was ready to go to Barrow, in time, he hoped, to let Jarvis know that the emergency arrangements at Point Hope would not be necessary. As Bertholf boarded the *Bear*, both he and Tuttle could not help but reflect upon the fact that it had been exactly seven months since the captain had put him, Jarvis, and Dr. Call ashore at Cape Vancouver.

Now it was full steam ahead for Point Barrow — or so Tuttle and Bertholf hoped. But on July 18, as he was nearing Port Lay, Tuttle once again ran into heavy ice and was forced to drop anchor. As he was gazing ahead, hoping to sight a clear channel through the ice that would allow him to get under way again, Tuttle spotted a local boat called a umiak picking its way through the ice floes toward the *Bear*. Aboard the umiak were the sunken *Orca's* captain, Albert Sherman; six of the whalemen; two native Alaskans; and Charlie Brower's assistant Fred Hopson.

Once aboard the *Bear*, they had much to tell. Jarvis, they stated, had begun to have serious doubts as to when the *Bear* would be able to reach Point Barrow. Even with the deer, he was concerned that all the various types of supplies he needed to sustain all those at Point Barrow and all those aboard the ships would run out. That is why, they explained, Jarvis had ordered Bertholf to Point Hope. And that was why Jarvis had asked them to try to make a 220-mile trip down what he hoped would be a narrow channel of open water between the ice and the shore all the way to Port Lay. There, Jarvis had hoped, they would find Tuttle and the *Bear*. It had, the men reported, been a harrowing trip, but they had made it, and miraculously they had found the *Bear*.

Then they handed Tuttle the letter from Jarvis they had been sent to deliver. In it, Jarvis stated that if the *Bear* did not reach Point Barrow by August 1, all those there would be in dire need. The letter then went on to explain that if the *Bear* had not arrived by that date, Jarvis would begin sending

Months after the snow at Charlie Brower's whaling station had melted, the stranded whalers were still waiting for the Bear *to arrive.*

the whalemen down the coast seeking whatever refuge they could find.

In all his many years in the Rescue Cutter Service, Captain Francis Tuttle had never felt such a sense of urgency. He simply had to reach Point Barrow by August 1. As he looked all around him, he saw nothing but ice, but he was determined to steam his way through. On July 22, he lifted his anchor and tried to fight his way free. The *Bear* hardly moved. The next day he tried again, but with little more success. On July 25, his spirits were lifted when he spotted open passages between the ever-shifting floes. But just as he was beginning to make headway, fog settled in so thickly that he could see almost nothing ahead of him, and he was forced to drop anchor again. Finally the fog lifted, and he was able to get fully under way. By late evening of the twenty-seventh, despite continually having to dodge dangerous floating ice, Tuttle had passed both Cape Belcher and Point Franklin. Then, navigating by the light of the summer Arctic midnight sun, Tuttle suddenly heard the crewman on watch cry out. He had spotted a ship that seemed locked in the ice some ten miles distant. As he gazed to where his lookout was pointing, Tuttle saw that it was the *Belvedere*. Having no idea what conditions on that stranded ship were like, he sent some of his men ashore with a generous supply of food. As soon as the provisions were piled high at a spot on the beach where the *Belvedere*'s crew were sure to see them, Tuttle hurried on.

"How well I remember July 28, 1898!" James Allen would write. "Smoke [from a ship] was reported to the south. Everyone was guessing what ship [it was]. Finally the masts were sighted and then the yards. It turned out to be that grand old revenue cutter U.S.S. *Bear,* to me one of the most beautiful ships that was ever built."

It was indeed the *Bear*. At 5 a.m., Tuttle sighted the whaling station. What amazed him was that there was still some heavy ice, some of it as much as thirty feet thick, protruding from the shore. Not daring to get closer than a mile from the beach, he ordered his ship to a halt. Just fifteen minutes later, he spotted a procession of men hurrying toward him. It was Jarvis, followed by a long line of whalemen fairly dancing across the ice. Their rescue ship had arrived, and they were about to go home.

Some of the photographs taken while those at Point Barrow awaited rescue were truly outstanding. Here, the remarkable amount of ice still present in August is revealed, while in the distance, the Fearless *and the recently arrived* Bear *try to fight their way out of entrapment.*

Well before the whaling fleet had become entrapped and the unprecedented rescue mission had been launched, the Bear *had compiled a proud history. The ship's heroic role in fulfilling President William McKinley's improbable orders would add immeasurably to her glory.*

Epilogue

The final chapter of the rescue of the whalers would not be accomplished without its anxious and potentially disastrous moments. Captain Tuttle had had a devil of a time getting to Point Barrow. He came excruciatingly close to not being able to get out.

Even as both the rescued and the rescuers were making their final preparations for leaving, heavy ice began building up and surrounding the *Bear*. "On August 1," Lieutenant Bertholf would later write, "the *Bear* was jammed tight up against the ground-ice by the pack, and we were in the same position as the vessels the previous fall. . . . The only thing we could do now was to look out for the crush and wait patiently for an easterly wind to carry the pack-ice [away]."

Two days later, near disaster struck. "On August 3," Bertholf would write, "the wind chopped around to the southwest, disturbed the pack, and brought on a pressure, so that our port side was pushed in a few inches. The snapping, cracking, and grinding of the timbers is a frightful sound, and for a few minutes it looked as if the stanch old *Bear,* that had seen so many cruises to the Arctic, was at last to leave her bones there, but fortunately the pressure ceased before any real damage was done. The danger was not over, however, for with the wind [still] blowing . . . [a repeat of what had just happened] was likely to occur at any time, and it was almost sure that the next time the *Bear* was doomed. Provisions were hastily gotten up and all preparations made to abandon her should it become necessary. For the next few days no one went asleep without expecting to be called at any time, and every morning we gave a sigh of relief to find the good old ship still safe."

For the next full week, Captain Tuttle tried everything he could to free his ship, including setting explosives in hope of blasting a passage through the ice. But nothing worked. His frustration heightened when he became aware that farther out at sea, the ice had broken up, finally releasing all the long-imprisoned whaleships. How ironic, he thought. The ships and crew members he had come to rescue were ready to sail home, and he was still trapped.

Finally, things began to change. On August 14, the wind shifted and the ice surrounding the *Bear* began to break up. Confident that the ship was finally about to free itself, he sent word for Jarvis, Call, and the whalemen to make their way to the *Bear*. Two days later, with the vessel now filled with humanity from bow to stern, more progress was made. "The pack," Bertholf wrote, "had by this time loosened sufficiently to allow the *Bear* to move back and forward a little, so steam was made on all her boilers, and she began to force her way through, but it took all the forenoon, backing and filling under a full head of steam, to get clear. About noon on the 16th, after a final rush at the barrier of ice, the *Bear* forced through, and we sent up a rousing cheer as we found ourselves in open water once more."

At one point in his struggle with the ice, Captain Tuttle became so concerned with his situation that he ordered the Bear's *records and other valuables thrown out on the floes in case the ship went down.*

On August 23, Tuttle put into Cape Prince of Wales for refueling. As soon as he had docked, Tom Lopp came aboard for a visit, where he was warmly greeted by Jarvis, Call, and Bertholf. It was a poignant moment. All four men had been instrumental in the remarkable rescue. Yet, they all realized that this was the only time in the entire adventure that all four had been in the same place at the same time.

On September 13, 1898, almost ten months after its feverish departure the previous December, the *Bear* arrived back in Seattle. But not to the type of homecoming one might have expected. When word of the whalemen's desperate plight was first made known,

the front pages of the nation's newspapers had been filled with pleas for the whalers' rescue, as impossible a task as it seemed to be. These pleas continued to dominate the papers' news coverage for days, and in some cases, for weeks. Now the miracle had taken place. The whalemen had been saved. It was an incredible story, but amazingly, there were no headlines. There were no front-page stories. Those newspapers that did report what had happened relegated their accounts to the back pages of the paper.

There was a reason. During the long months that the rescue efforts were taking place, an event of worldwide magnitude had fully captured the nation's attention. The United States had gone to war with Spain. Every day, the country's newspapers were filled with accounts of the Spanish-American War—stories of the exploits of Teddy Roosevelt and his Rough Riders,

The Bear *finally breaks free of the ice. Years later, writing of the ship's ordeal in leaving Point Barrow, Brower would declare that "that, I think, was the closest shave the old cutter ever had."*

accounts of Admiral George Dewey's victory at Manila Bay. America's appetite for news of the war and its heroes was insatiable. There was little room for anything else.

Fortunately, however, there were those who were aware of and fully appreciative of what had taken place in the Arctic. Among them was President William McKinley, the man who had launched the great adventure in the North. In a special message to the United States Congress, McKinley paid tribute to those who had risked and endured so much. "The hardships and perils encountered by the members of the overland expedition in their great journey through the almost uninhabited region, a barrier waste of ice and snow, facing death itself every day for . . . months, over a route never before traveled by white men," the president proclaimed, "all make another glorious page in the history of American seamen."

In his final report of the rescue, Captain Francis Tuttle would state, "With a herd of over 400 reindeer to drive and care for, they pushed their way through what at times seemed impassible obstacles, across frozen seas, and over snow-clad mountains, with tireless energy until Point Barrow was reached and the object of the expedition successfully accomplished."

Dr. Sheldon Jackson, the man who had been most instrumental in introducing reindeer into Alaska, was particularly awestruck by what the members of the Overland Relief Expedition had accomplished. And he was dismayed by the way the press had practically ignored the achievement. "Had not the events of the . . . war distracted the attention of the nation," he wrote, "this wonderful trip of 2,000 miles overland, north of the arctic circle in midwinter, would have filled the columns of the newspapers on this continent and in Europe. Because [it occurred] at a time when other events claimed the attention of the public, it is no less deserving of its reward."

Eventually, Lieutenant David Jarvis, Lieutenant Ellsworth Bertholf, and Dr. Samuel Call would be awarded Congressional Gold Medals, one of the highest honors the United States could bestow. Together with others, not the least of which were the indigenous people of the North, they had lived an unforgettable story.

ARCTIC
OCEAN

RUSSIA

Fearless
Rosario   *Newport*
Belvedere   *Jeannie*
Orca   Point
Jesse H. Freeman   Barrow
Station

Kobokik

Pitmegea River

Point Hope Whaling Station

Kivalina River

Kotzebue Sound   Cape Blossom

Escholtz Bay

Cape Prince of Wales

Port Clarence

Golovnin Bay

Cape
Rodney

Norton Sound

Unalakleet

St. Michael

BERING
SEA

ST. LAWRENCE ISLAND

Ki-yi-lieug-a-mute

Cape
Vancouver

Tununak

NUNIVAK
ISLAND

ALASKA

KLONDIKE REGION

Wanderer   HERSCHEL
ISLAND

Yukon River

GULF OF ALASKA

N
E
W
S

NORTH PACIFIC
OCEAN

Dutch Harbor

from Seattle
to Seattle

.... Jarvis and Call

——— Lopp

– – – Bertholf on land

— – The *Bear* and Bertholf

——— The *Bear*'s summer route

- - - - The *Bear*'s winter route

——— The *Bear*'s return home

Further Information

What Happened to Them

CHARLIE ARTISARLOOK

Charlie Artisarlook's accomplishments both before and during the rescue of the stranded whalers were instrumental in proving to doubters that those who were native to the frozen North were fully capable of owning and managing their own reindeer herds. Tragically, less than two years after returning home from delivering the herd to Point Barrow, Charlie Artisarlook died in a measles epidemic.

THE BEAR

From the time that it brought the rescued whalemen back to Seattle until well into the 1900s, the *Bear* continued to patrol Alaskan waters, providing aid to mariners and to people living along the coast. When it was put into dry dock in the late 1920s, it appeared that the ship's days at sea were finally over. But destiny still had many new adventures in store for the *Bear*. Purchased by famed explorer Admiral Richard Byrd, the *Bear* carried Byrd and his party on two historic trips to Antarctica, first in 1933–34 and then in 1939–41. When the United States entered World War II in 1941, the *Bear* was again pressed into service patrolling the waters off Greenland and Iceland.

Soon after the war ended in 1945, the ship was dry-docked once again, this time in Halifax, Nova Scotia. But in 1963, she was purchased by a businessman from Philadelphia who intended to turn her into a floating restaurant. Almost as if in protest of such a degrading ending to such a proud and heroic past, the *Bear*'s old seams opened up while she was being towed to Philadelphia and the eighty-nine-year-old vessel sank in three hundred feet of water. Despite a lengthy underwater search headed by the man who had discovered the remains of the famous Civil War ironclad vessel the *Monitor,* the *Bear* was never found. "She still lies in that watery grave," former dean of the Coast Guard Academy David Sandell has stated, "perhaps a fitting place for one with so grand a seagoing history."

ELLSWORTH BERTHOLF

Ellsworth Bertholf did not have to wait long after returning from the rescue of the whalers at Point Barrow to embark on another adventure. In the winter of 1901, the United States Department of the Interior asked him to travel to Siberia to purchase a breed of reindeer that was larger and hardier than the deer that had been previously brought to northern Alaska.

Seven years after this accomplishment, Bertholf realized one of his fondest dreams when he was appointed captain of the *Bear*. The man who, previous to his participation in the Overland Relief Expedition, had never been in the Arctic then spent three years patrolling the Bering Sea and other Arctic waters. In 1911, Bertholf received an even greater promotion when he was appointed by President William Howard Taft to serve as captain-commandant of the entire Revenue Cutter Service.

Even greater glory lay ahead. On January 28, 1915, the Revenue Cutter Service and the United States Life-Saving Service were combined into a new military entity. President Woodrow Wilson not only accepted Bertholf's suggestion that the new service be called the United States Coast Guard but also appointed Bertholf its first commandant. It was here that Bertholf made some of his most important contributions of all. The Coast Guard was formed as World War I was being waged. The new commandant not only steered the brand-new service through the trials of the world's first global war but also earned the title of "the savior of the Coast Guard" by successfully overcoming the efforts of members of Congress and certain military leaders to have the Coast Guard absorbed by either the Navy or the Marine Corps.

Ellsworth Bertholf retired in 1919 but remained active as the first vice-president of the American Bureau of Shipping. He died in New York City in 1921.

CHARLES BROWER

After a lengthy period of negotiations with government authorities, Charles Brower was finally paid what was due to him for helping to sustain the stranded whalemen at Point Barrow.

After this unpleasant experience, Brower returned to Point Barrow, where he would become the most famous citizen of the frozen Arctic wilderness. Fondly known both as "the northernmost white man" and "king of the Arctic," Brower spent the rest of his long life at Point Barrow, where he played host to such notables as Roald Amundsen, the first man to sail completely through the Northwest Passage, and to hundreds of whaling captains and crews, whom he described as "men the like of whom the world has never known."

Along with continuing his successful whaling operations, Brower would serve as United States Commissioner to Alaska and Alaskan postmaster. Brower married a native woman named Asinnataq, with whom he raised a large family. Several of his children became leading citizens of Alaska and, like their father, great champions of native Alaskans.

In the early 1940s, displaying a flair for writing that few who knew him realized he had, Brower wrote a book titled *Fifty Years Below Zero: A Lifetime of Adventure in the Far North,* which became a best seller. Ending his book with what was nothing short of an anthem to his love of the Arctic, Brower wrote, "It's the long winter nights that bring the past to life. Nights when the North Pole sends a gale howling around Barrow and I sit snugly working on my specimens, or writing, or carving a bit of ivory. Or perhaps saying to myself, as we used to in the old days, 'But just wait till next spring!'

"For on such a night familiar echoes come easily to the ear of memory; ghostly sounds which, nevertheless, will always typify the Arctic to me. I hear them plainly as I work—the rhythmic beat of the [Eskimo's] drum, wind-swept shouts of a triumphant crew, or, mingling with the boom of ice, the dying *swis-s-sh* of a bowhead whale."

DR. SAMUEL CALL

In 1899, a year after returning from Point Barrow, Dr. Samuel Call resigned from the Revenue Cutter Service and set up a private medical practice in Nome, Alaska. Thanks to a gold rush, the once tiny settlement of Nome had turned into a town, and was soon to be a city of twenty thousand people. Because of unsanitary conditions and disease, it was also a community in desperate need of medical help. Call remained in Nome for almost four years, not only maintaining his private practice but also serving as the community's health officer.

While in Nome, Call also undertook another incredible journey. It came about when a Catholic priest named Father Jacquet became insane and needed to be taken for help to a mission at the Alaskan settlement of Holy Cross, a round-trip trek of more than 1,200 miles. Volunteering to deliver the priest on what he regarded as an errand of mercy, Call told a reporter before leaving that it was potentially an even more dangerous journey than that of the Overland Relief Expedition.

In 1903, after leaving Nome, Call rejoined the Cutter Service and served first on the ship *Thetis* and later on the *McCulloch*. His extraordinary adventures, however, had taken their toll, and in 1908 he was forced to retire. A year later, at the age of fifty, he died in Hollister, California.

DAVID JARVIS

Lieutenant David Jarvis had barely been back in Seattle when he was appointed to succeed the retiring Francis Tuttle as captain of the *Bear*. And within weeks he was back in the Arctic, taking the *Bear* north on its regular trip.

Throughout the entire period that the whalers had been stranded at Point Barrow, another momentous happening was taking place in the frozen North. Gold had been discovered in the northern portion of the Seward Peninsula, and, as had been the case in the historic Gold Rush of 1849, tens of thousands of people had dropped everything and, by any means possible, made their way to Alaska, seeking to get rich. Very few found gold. Most found themselves caught in a hostile environment in real danger of perishing from the elements or from disease.

When Jarvis reached Cape Prince of Wales, he learned that some five hundred of the would-be miners had wintered near Kotzebue Sound, where they hoped to find gold. He was told that many of these people were in desperate condition. When he steamed on to where they were encamped, he found the situation even worse than he feared. As many as one hundred had died of starvation, disease, or drowning. After relieving as much of the distress as possible by leaving medicine, food, and other supplies, Jarvis transported more than eighty of the most ill or weakened people to the safety of St. Michael. He then headed the *Bear* back to the encampment, where he took aboard many of the healthier gold seekers who now wished to be taken back home.

Jarvis's continued heroic actions captured the attention of President William McKinley's successor, President Theodore Roosevelt, and in 1900, Roosevelt appointed him customs collector of Alaska. Five years later, the president asked Jarvis to become governor of the Alaskan territory. But by this time, Jarvis had plans of his own. He had spent most of his life serving his country, the whalers, and the native people of the North. Now he felt it was time to build a personal fortune by taking advantage of the many commercial opportunities he saw developing in Alaska.

With the same energy he had brought to his Revenue Cutter Service career, Jarvis became involved at a high level in private salmon canning, fisheries, and mining operations in Alaska and in financial investment dealings in Seattle. All of these activities, however, involved politics and, in many cases, shady dealings. By 1910, Jarvis and many of his business associates found themselves caught up in scandal, accused of bribery and other forms of corruption.

For a man who had become accustomed to honor and acclaim, it was too much. On June 23, 1911, David Jarvis committed suicide by shooting himself in a room at the Seattle Athletic Club. Lying in the room was an envelope on the back of which he had written, "tired and worn out." He was only fifty-eight years old.

Jarvis's tragic, self-imposed ending, however, could not diminish all that he had accomplished. In 1903, a 5,000-foot-high mountain, located in Wrangell–St. Elias National Park in eastern Alaska, was named for him. In 1972, the United States Coast Guard's newest and most advanced 378-foot-high ice-breaking vessel was named the USCGC *Jarvis*. And to this day, one of the Coast Guard's most prestigious honors is the Jarvis Award, given for "inspirational leadership."

TOM LOPP

In what amounted to a gross injustice, Tom Lopp never received from the government the honor or the recognition that was due him for the vital role that he played in the Overland Relief Expedition. Unlike Jarvis, Call, or Bertholf, he received no medal for bravery. But that did not deter him from becoming a pivotal figure in Alaskan history.

For almost thirty-five years after returning home from his harrowing journey to Point Barrow, Lopp unselfishly devoted himself to promoting the raising of reindeer as a way for the indigenous people to improve their economic life and to providing increased educational opportunities for the natives. Displaying extraordinary passion for these causes, Lopp served as chief of the Alaskan division of the United States Bureau of Education, superintendent of reindeer for the northern district of Alaska, and as reindeer expert for the Hudson's Bay Company.

More than any other individual, Lopp was responsible for improving conditions in the coastal villages of Alaska. Among many other contributions to the welfare of the people who lived there, he was responsible for the establishment of sixty-six native schools and five hospitals. A leading champion of native rights, he created the *Eskimo Bulletin,* the first newspaper devoted to issues concerning the indigenous people.

It was not until he died, in 1939, that Tom Lopp finally received the recognition he deserved. Among the tributes he received was that from a United States Coast Guard lieutenant commander who wrote, "Scrupulously honest, untiring in his efforts, far-sighted, and guided by his love for his fellow man, he has unselfishly blazed the most difficult trails, has overcome conditions seemingly [i]nsurmountable, and will go down in Alaskan history as her Lincoln." Lopp Lagoon, an eighteen-mile-long bay near where Lopp established the first reindeer station outside of Siberia, is named for him.

NED MCILHENNY

When Ned McIlhenny finally departed from Point Barrow, he brought back with him a staggering eleven tons of bird eggs, animal skins, skeletons, and artifacts, which were delivered to the University of Pennsylvania's Natural History Museum.

Immediately after returning to Louisiana, McIlhenny took over the reins of the family's Tabasco sauce company. Displaying the same energy he had devoted to his Arctic exploits, he expanded the business, applied new marketing techniques, and made *Tabasco* a household word. In the process he won a court battle that resulted in the company gaining the sole right to the Tabasco trademark.

But, successful as he was at growing the family business, he found that he had developed a new passion — conservation. Even before he had left for Point Barrow, he had become alarmed at how one of his favorite creatures, the beautiful snowy egret, which had once lived near his home by the thousands, was becoming extinct. "This great reduction," he wrote, was "not due to natural causes, but to the persecution of [the egrets] by man, who has killed them for both sport and profit." McIlhenny particularly blamed what he called "plume hunters," who killed as many of the egrets as they could for their long feathers, which women of the day loved to wear in their hats. The women themselves did not escape McIlhenny's wrath, and he condemned them for their "barbaric love of adornment, which 1,800 years of Christian civilization had failed to eradicate."

McIlhenny did much more than bemoan what was happening to the egrets; he did something about it. Both his home and his business were located on Louisiana's Avery Island, where he built a sanctuary, which he called Bird City, whose main purpose was to care for egrets, protect them from harm, and save them from extinction. President Theodore Roosevelt, widely regarded as the "father of American conservationism," called Bird City "the most noteworthy reserve in the country." For the rest of his life, McIlhenny, as busy as he was, would find the time to study and save bird life. It is estimated that over a forty-year period, he personally banded more than 285,000 birds.

And he did not stop there. Buoyed by the success of Bird City, McIlhenny began purchasing enormous tracts of land — almost one million acres in all — in other wilderness areas of Louisiana and turning them into wildlife sanctuaries. When he found that he could not personally afford certain of these purchases, he convinced some of the wealthiest individuals in America to help finance them.

As if all this were not enough, McIlhenny also transformed his personal 250-acre estate, which he called Jungle Gardens, into a nursery that included 60 varieties of bamboo, 150 varieties of camellias, and 1,700 different kinds of irises, many of which he had introduced to the world through his own experimentation. Given all these interests, it was not surprising that McIlhenny also published several books, with titles such as *The Autobiography of an Egret*, *The Alligator's Life History*, and *Bird City*. Ned McIlhenny died in 1949 at the age of seventy-seven.

REINDEER

When the *Bear* arrived to pick up the whalers and their rescuers, there were 391 reindeer remaining at Point Barrow, 201 from the original herd and 190 fawns that had been born after the herd had been delivered. The deer that had been slaughtered had provided some 12,500 pounds of fresh meat for the whalers, making it possible, in Jarvis's words, "to bring the men through without extreme suffering and sickness." It was decided that the remaining reindeer should be given to Dr. Marsh at the Presbyterian mission to benefit the indigenous people at Point Barrow. By this time Jarvis, like Tom Lopp, had become a firm believer in the value of reindeer in improving the indigenous people's well-being. "The whole coast is well adapted for them," he wrote, "and I know nothing that would be so beneficial as their introduction in large numbers through out all the northern part of Alaska."

The reindeer's role in the rescue of the whalemen drew attention to these unique animals. In the decade that followed the rescue, many voices spoke out predicting how profoundly the raising of reindeer would benefit the native-born people of Alaska. Others saw a whole new value in the deer. "The day is coming," author Frank Carpenter wrote, "when reindeer meat will be sold in our American markets just like beef and mutton. This reindeer meat will come from Alaska." By 1930, the number of deer in Alaska had risen to some 250,000.

All such predictions, however, proved to be false. The government was unable to develop an effective system by which the native population, widely scattered throughout a vast area, could herd and care for reindeer in enormous numbers. At the same time, private companies, which had no interest in the natives' well-being but sought to reap profits in the animals' potential as a major food source, began to take over the reindeer industry. Their hopes were dashed when the American public never developed a taste for reindeer meat. Today, there are less than 20,000 reindeer in Alaska, and the number grows smaller every year.

GEORGE FRED TILTON

George Fred Tilton, the *Belvedere*'s mate who had been sent out by his fellow stranded whalers on the one-in-a-million chance he might make it all the way to a

West Coast port and seek aid, continued his extraordinary journey after his unexpected encounter with David Jarvis. In many ways, this part of his travels was even more remarkable than all he had endured before meeting Jarvis.

After leaving Jarvis, Tilton, battling through yet another series of blizzards, reached St. Michael. Ten days later, after crossing mountain ranges through storms that destroyed some of his dogs, he and the guides who accompanied him arrived at Andreafski. When he sought to purchase the fresh team of dogs that he needed to carry on, the traders in the village, knowing his desperation, set a price on the dogs much higher than Tilton could afford to pay.

Fortunately, a Moravian missionary, sympathetic to what Tilton was trying to accomplish, stepped in and not only supplied the whaler with new dogs but also guided him all the way to Katmai, a village on the Shelikof Strait, more than four hundred miles away. When Tilton arrived at Katmai, he found that the only boat available was an old, damaged, small fishing vessel. Refusing to give up this far along, he mended the boat as best he could and then managed to take it across the turbulent and dangerous water of the Shelikof Strait to Kodiak Island. At Kodiak, he was able to secure passage on a steamboat, which arrived in Portland, Oregon, on April 8, 1898.

Tilton had been absolutely convinced that Jarvis had no chance of accomplishing his mission. The irony of his almost unbelievable journey was that by the time he arrived in Portland, the Overland Relief Expedition had reached Point Barrow and the rescue of the whalemen was well under way. But that does not diminish the courage and determination displayed in his heroic attempt to give his fellow whalers what he thought was their only chance for survival.

Tilton would return to whaling and would eventually become captain of the *Belvedere*. Later he would distinguish himself as an officer in the United States Navy. He would spend the last years of his career in a most rewarding way. As curator aboard the *Charles W. Morgan*, the last of the great whaling ships, which had been put on display in New Bedford before being permanently moved to Mystic Seaport, he spent hours telling stories of the glory days of whaling. Most interesting of all the stories, the majority of the thousands of visitors agreed, were Tilton's accounts of his own remarkable adventures.

Timeline

September 10–September 28, 1897

Eight whaleships with more than 265 men aboard become locked in the ice off Point Barrow, Alaska. Two of the ships are destroyed by the ice.

Mid-October, 1897

The ship *Alexander* arrives in San Francisco with news of the whalers' desperate plight.

November 15, 1897

Treasury Secretary Lyman Gage relays President William McKinley's orders that a rescue mission be launched.

November 27, 1897

The Revenue Cutter Service ship *Bear,* with the Overland Relief Expedition members aboard, leaves Seattle for the Arctic.

December 13, 1897

Heavy ice prevents the *Bear* from putting the members of the rescue party ashore at Cape Prince of Wales.

December 16, 1897

The *Bear* lands the rescue party ashore near the village of Tununak.

December 18, 1897

Jarvis, Call, Bertholf, and other members of the rescue mission set out from Tununak.

December 21, 1897

Jarvis orders Bertholf to remain at the village of Ki-yi-lieug-a-mute to acquire fresh dogs.

December 22, 1897

The *Bear* puts into Dutch Harbor, Alaska, for the winter.

December 30, 1897

Jarvis and Call reach St. Michael.

January 1, 1898

Jarvis leaves a note for Bertholf instructing him to join Jarvis and Call at Unalakleet with fresh dogs.

January 3, 1898

Jarvis and Call encounter George Fred Tilton.

January 5, 1898

Jarvis leaves a note for Bertholf ordering him to take the supplies he has purchased at Unalakleet and transport them to Cape Blossom for the final leg of the rescue mission to Point Barrow.

January 12, 1898

Jarvis and Call acquire sled reindeer at Golovnin Bay.

January 14, 1898

Jarvis has two near disasters with his reindeer sled.

January 19, 1898

Jarvis and Call reach Charlie Artisarlook's reindeer station at Cape Rodney.

January 24, 1898

Jarvis, Call, and Artisarlook reach Tom Lopp's reindeer station at Cape Prince of Wales.

February 3, 1898

Jarvis, Call, Lopp, and the deer herd set out for Point Barrow.

February 5, 1898

Jarvis and Call leave Lopp and the herd and head for Kotzebue Sound.

February 6, 1898

Jarvis and Call encounter the native Perninyuk and hire him to guide them to Cape Blossom.

February 11, 1898

After a long and dangerous journey, Bertholf arrives with the supplies at Samms's mission at Cape Blossom.

February 12, 1898

Jarvis and Call cross Kotzebue Sound and arrive at Samms's mission, where they find Bertholf and the supplies.

February 16, 1898

Jarvis and Call trek to Point Hope seeking news of the stranded whalers.

February 20, 1898

At Point Hope, Jarvis and Call learn of the whalers' deteriorating condition.

February 26, 1898

After leaving Point Hope, Jarvis finds Lopp and the herd at the Kivalina River.

March 6, 1898

Traveling separately, Jarvis and Call and Lopp and the herd head for Point Barrow.

March 25, 1898

Jarvis and Call reach the *Belvedere*.

March 29, 1898

Jarvis and Call arrive at Point Barrow.

March 30, 1898

Lopp and the reindeer herd arrive at Point Barrow.

June 14, 1898

The *Bear* leaves its winter quarters and heads for Point Barrow.

July 2, 1898

A huge storm strikes Point Barrow, destroying the *Rosario*.

July 19, 1898

Captain Tuttle and the *Bear* encounter men from Point Barrow sent by Jarvis with the news that help must arrive by August 1.

July 27, 1898

The *Bear* spots the *Belvedere* and leaves supplies for its crew.

July 28, 1898

The *Bear* reaches Point Barrow.

August 1–August 15, 1898

With those who have been stranded at Point Barrow waiting to board her, the *Bear* finds itself trapped in the ice.

August 16, 1898

The *Bear* finally breaks free of the ice and heads home with the whalers and the men of the Overland Relief Expedition.

September 13, 1898

The *Bear* arrives in Seattle.

Source Notes

A page reference in italics indicates caption text.

Key to abbreviations:

ISEGR: Institute of Social, Economic, and Government Research

Overland Expedition Report: *Report of the Cruise of the U.S. Revenue Cutter* Bear *and the Overland Expedition for the Relief of the Whalers in the Arctic Ocean*

Chapter One: Stranded

p. xii: "Never in all . . . which they sailed." Everett S. Allen, p. 159.

p. 1: "We have to . . . bad this year." Log of the *Alexander.*

p. 2: "This went on . . . a dangerous position." Arthur James Allen, p. 48.

p. 2: "Back and forth . . . strain much longer" and "I can tell you . . . happy set of men." Taliaferro, p. 195.

p. 2: "In their search . . . of the Indies." Ellis, p. ix.

p. 4: "we expect to obtain . . . from our explorations." Bernard, p. 105.

p. 4: "For me the real . . . is absolutely unknown." Ibid., p.106.

p. 6: "was here to . . . collecting shipwrecked sailors?" Brower, p. 201.

p. 7: "A sorry-looking . . . contest for them." Arthur James Allen, p. 224.

p. 7: "Mr. Denny, the chief . . . was slow work." Ibid., p. 56.

p. 8: "At nine o'clock . . . face and hands." Bernard, p. 109.

p. 9: "The house would . . . sickness and death." Arthur James Allen, p. 64.

p. 9: "As soon as . . . shifted to me." Taliaferro, pp. 271–272.

p. 10: "This morning I . . . or sixty below?" Bernard, p. 110.

p. 11: "Last night . . . by this decision." Taliaferro, p. 274.

p. 11: "I told her . . . had no proof." Brower, p. 275.

Chapter Two: An Audacious Plan

p. 14: "The best information . . . to the rescue." Overland Expedition Report, p. 5.

p. 14: "The first and . . . on the hoof." Ibid., p. 6.

p. 16: "Fogs are frequent . . . their own vessel." Starbuck, p. 99.

p. 16: "I long for . . . you are worshipped." Berton, p. 253.

p. 17: "When the cabin . . . small ice floe." McKinley, p. 48.

p 17: "Any Arctic whaleman . . . the country impassable." Tilton, p. 171.

p. 19: "If you are . . . question your courage." Overland Expedition Report, p. 74.

p. 20: "as a boy . . . reach the ocean." Kroll, p. 3.

p. 20: "the spirit which . . . through life." Ibid., p. 3.

p. 22: "It is extremely . . . only eighteen days." Bertholf, p. 4.

p. 24: "On the morning . . . make its appearance." Ibid., p. 4.

p. 24: "Knowing that as . . . full speed [south]." Overland Expedition Report, p. 13.

p. 24: "At the time . . . for Cape Vancouver." Bertholf, p. 4.

pp. 24–25: "The beach at . . . unfit for use." Overland Expedition Report, p. 29.

p. 25: "We stood on . . . our friends again." Bertholf, p. 4.

Chapter Three: The Long Trek Begins

p. 27: "The Alaskan sleds . . . spilling the load." Bertholf, pp. 5–6.

pp. 27–28: "Our camp-gear . . . fatigue of travelling." Ibid., pp. 7–8.

pp. 28–29: "The first day . . . deep valley between." Ibid., p. 6.

p. 30: "There was no . . . here and there." Ibid., pp. 8–9.

p. 30: "I have seen . . . signs of fatigue." Ibid., p. 6.

pp. 30–31: "These huts are . . . the outer entrance." Ibid., p. 7.

p. 32: "The hospitality of . . . finished our meal." Overland Expedition Report, p. 65.

p. 32: "[Kalenin] informed us . . . the same thing." Ibid., p. 35.

p. 34: "Before the *Bear* . . . directed to them." Ibid., p. 39.

Chapter Four: An Extraordinary Encounter

p. 37: "It was necessary . . . far north as [the approaches to Point Barrow]." Overland Expedition Report, p. 42.

p. 38: "It is characteristic . . . to its dangers." Ibid., p. 70.

pp. 38–39: "On starting out . . . warm air in." Ibid., p. 53.

p. 39: "It is always . . . fire for tea." Ibid., p. 76.

p. 40: "Our road was . . . we had accomplished." Ibid., p. 44.

p. 40: "a white whaler-man" and "from the ship." Tilton, p. 208.

p. 43: "found that our . . . guarantee of relief." Ibid., pp. 183–184.

p. 43: "It was then . . . a whaling voyage." Ibid., p. 185.

p. 43: "Many of the . . . such trying conditions." Ibid., p. 183.

p. 44: "delighted to know . . . never reach there." Ibid., p. 207.

Chapter Five: Blizzards, Reindeer, and Near Disaster

p. 48: "Most everyone of . . . alone their clothes." Arthur James Allen, p. 64.

p. 50: "Sir, I enclose . . . send to you." Bixby, pp. 163–164.

p. 50: "The runners would . . . to drag along." Overland Expedition Report, pp. 45–46.

pp. 51–52: "[The deer] are harnessed . . . quiet and control." Ibid., p. 47.

p. 52: "All hands must . . . in the snow." Ibid., p. 47.

p. 53: "bolted down the . . . even for contemplation." Ibid., pp. 48–49.

p. 54: "It was impossible . . . to help myself." Ibid., p. 48–49.

p. 54: "made the best . . . for the night" and "In an hour . . . hands and knees " Ibid., p. 49.

p. 55: "The gale still . . . there another day." Ibid., p. 49.

p. 55: "We hoped to . . . it from freezing." Ibid., p. 50.

Chapter Six: A Desperate Request

p. 56: "From whatever . . . for Point Barrow." Ibid., pp. 8–9.

p. 57: "I had looked . . . task it brought." Overland Expedition Report, p. 50.

p. 59: "Jarvis knew well . . . condition of the unfortunate [whalemen]." Taliaferro, pp. 234–235.

p. 59: "I explained to . . . own free will." Overland Expedition Report, p. 51.

p. 59: "tell Mr. Jarvis . . . will we do?" Taliaferro, p. 235.

pp. 60–61: "If you will . . . that doubtful drive." Ibid., p. 245.

p. 61: "I had dreaded . . . men in distress." Overland Expedition Report, p. 51.

Chapter Seven: Another Agonizing Decision

p. 63: "I think the . . . on the expedition." Overland Expedition Report, p. 55.

p. 64: "the thermometer . . . still blowing." Ibid., p. 55.

p. 64: "About 8 o'clock . . . meant to freeze." Ibid., p. 54.

pp. 64–65: "Pushing and lifting . . . bag, and sleep." Ibid., pp. 54–55.

p. 65: "I thought the . . . violence of the work." Ibid., p. 55.

p. 66: "Mr. Lopp is . . . its speedy accomplishment." Ibid., p. 6.

p. 66: "was indispensable . . . in the country." Ibid., p. 56.

p. 66: "The early successes . . . form of wealth." ISEGR, p. 7.

p. 67: "Tom Gorrah" and "the good man." Carpenter, chapter 26.

p. 69: "You can imagine . . . in distress." Taliaferro, p. 240.

Chapter Eight: Bertholf Battles the Odds

pp. 72–73: "We were off . . . to feel cold." Bertholf, p. 7.

p. 73: "Under ordinary circumstances . . . in this climate." Overland Expedition
    Report, p. 103.

p. 73: "I was not . . . medicines with me." Ibid., p. 105.

p. 74: "As Alexis had . . . further his recovery." Ibid., p. 105.

pp. 75–76: "Although [Unalakleet] is . . . the difficult trail." Bertholf, p. 14.

p. 77: "Our guide led . . . the little fellows." Ibid., p. 15.

p. 78: "One of us . . . took its place." Ibid., p. 14.

p. 78: "After the meal . . . air as possible." Ibid., p. 15.

p. 79: "I was obliged . . . across the country." Overland Expedition Report, p. 107.

pp. 79–81: "Having allowed the . . . a full stop." Ibid., pp. 107–108.

Chapter Nine: A Hazardous Crossing

p. 82: "It was blowing . . . reindeer parkas." Taliaferro, p. 27.

pp. 83–84: "The journey and . . . at Point Barrow." Overland Expedition Report,
    p. 57.

p. 84: "Things had now . . . not be foretold." Ibid., p. 57.

p. 84: "In this way . . . state of excitement." Bixby, p. 175.

p. 84: "This little fellow . . . one compact body." Overland Expedition Report,
    p. 58.

p. 85: "[Dr. Call] furnished much amusement . . . for some time." Taliaferro, p. 243.

p. 85: "We were not . . . to be hauled." Overland Expedition Report, p. 59.

pp. 87–88: "The natives along . . . at Cape Blossom." Ibid., pp. 60–61.

p. 88: "It was more . . . depended on them." Bixby, p. 178.

pp. 88–89: "All the next . . . on our side." Overland Expedition Report, p. 61.

Chapter Ten: Dire News of the Whalers

p. 91: "We were relieved . . . to Point Barrow." Overland Expedition Report, p. 63.

p. 91: "I paid off . . . our herders had [become worn out]." Ibid., pp. 63–64.

p. 92: "The difference between . . . his foot gear." Ibid., pp. 64–65.

p. 92: "It was reported . . . way to obtain." Ibid., p. 66.

p. 94: "almost dead from hunger and fatigue." Ibid., p. 67.

p. 95: "showed the marks . . . of Kotzebue Sound." Ibid., p. 67.

pp. 95–96: "had fully 400 miles . . . do it in." Ibid., p. 68.

pp. 96–97: "We had now come . . . dangers and menaces." Ibid., pp. 69–70.

p. 97: "We had been warned . . . on the road." Ibid., pp. 73–74.

p. 97: "We had now been traveling . . . warm air possible." Ibid., p. 75.

p. 98: "[I] looked anxiously . . . bread box, [with a sign upon it]" and "Letter
   between boards." Ibid., p. 183.

p. 98: "We were wet . . . with wet clothes." Ibid., p. 184.

p. 98: "It was all we could do . . . our fires going." Ibid., p. 73.

p. 99: "we could see . . . intense white snow." Bixby, p. 184.

Chapter Eleven: Contact

pp. 101–102: "The favorite way . . . not thought of." Overland Expedition Report,
   p. 74.

p. 102: "almost every twig . . . of your error." Ibid., p. 78.

p. 102:"We drew up . . . extended to us." Ibid., p. 79.

pp. 102–103: "Captain Millard was . . . end his misery." Ibid., pp. 79–80.

pp. 103–104: "We were so near . . . of our destination." Ibid., pp. 80–81.

pp. 104–105: "Passing rapidly by . . . the outside world." Ibid., p. 81.

p. 105: "when Lieutenant Jarvis . . . to help *us.*" Brower, p. 212.

Chapter Twelve: Jarvis Takes Charge

p. 107: "When the herd . . . that long journey." Overland Expedition Report, p. 84.

p. 108: "[the whalemen] were much debilitated . . . and exercise enforced." Ibid.,
   p. 83.

p. 109: "These quarters were . . . easily be inspected." Ibid., p. 84.

p. 109: "Provisions were short . . . along so far." Ibid., pp. 81–82.

pp. 109–110: "I found that the greatest . . . anywhere." Ibid., p. 99.

p. 110: "No one can . . . the right time." Arthur James Allen, p. 74.

p. 110: "At 12:45 p.m. . . . on the third day." Overland Expedition Report, p. 119.

p. 111: "Since most of . . . never forgot that." Brower, p. 214.

p. 111: "cleanliness was an absolute necessity." Overland Expedition Report,
     p. 85.

p. 112: "It was difficult . . . was greatly improved." Overland Expedition Report,
     p. 85.

p. 112: "Discipline and obedience . . . all knew that." Arthur James Allen, p. 75.

p. 113: "Aside from . . . disturbances and troubles." Overland Expedition Report,
     p. 89.

p. 113: "But for . . . to their relief." Bertholf, p. 19.

p. 114: "Louis Rich, carpenter . . . after that lesson." Overland Expedition
     Report, p. 90.

p. 114: "After getting the camp . . . the outlying vessels." Ibid., p. 86.

p. 114: "I started [out] with . . . arrived at the vessel." Ibid., p. 92.

pp. 114–115: "This . . . hauling was . . . grand beyond description." Ibid., p. 98.

p. 116: "They had a . . . very bad straits." Ibid., p. 88.

p. 117: "the arrival of . . . discipline until [the *Bear*'s] arrival." Ibid., p. 88.

p. 118: "He gave the . . . 10 miles away." Arthur James Allen, p. 75.

p. 118: "A Ball-game with . . . certainly a novelty." Bertholf, p. 22.

pp. 118–119: "There was nothing . . . got ashore safely." Overland Expedition
     Report, p. 98.

Chapter Thirteen: Voyage Against Time

p. 124: "How well I . . . was ever built." Arthur James Allen, pp. 83–84.

Epilogue

p. 127: "On August 1 . . . carry the pack-ice [away]." Bertholf, pp. 23–24.

pp. 127–128: "On August 3 . . . ship still safe." Ibid., p. 24.

p. 128: "The pack had . . . water once more." Ibid., p. 24.

p. *129:* "that, I think . . . cutter ever had." Brower, p. 215.

p. 130: "The hardships and . . . of American seamen." McKinley.

p. 130: "With a herd . . . successfully accomplished." Overland Expedition Report, p. 137.

p. 130: "Had not the . . . of its reward." Jackson, p. 29.

What Happened to Them

p. 135: "She still lies . . . a seagoing history." Sandell interview.

p. 137: "men the like . . . has never known." Brower, jacket flap.

p. 137: "It's the long . . . a bowhead whale." Ibid., p. 310.

p. 140: "Scrupulously honest, untiring . . . as her Lincoln." Taliaferro, p. 362.

p. 141: "This great reduction . . . sport and profit" and "barbaric love of . . . failed to eradicate." Bernard, p. 100.

p. 141: "father of American conservatism" and "the most . . . in the country." Ibid., p. 104.

p. 142: "to bring the . . . suffering and sickness." and "The whole coast . . . part of Alaska." Overland Expedition Report, p. 101.

p. 142: "The day is . . . come from Alaska." Carpenter, chapter 26.

Bibliography

Allen, Arthur James. *A Whaler & Trader in the Arctic, 1895 to 1944: My Life with the Bowhead.* Anchorage: Alaska Northwest Publishing Company, 1978.

Allen, Everett S. *Children of the Light.* Boston: Little, Brown, 1973.

Bernard, Shane K. *Tabasco: An Illustrated History.* Avery Island, LA: McIlhenny Company, 2007.

Bertholf, Ellsworth P. "The Rescue of the Whalers." *Harper's New Monthly Magazine,* June 1899.

Berton, Pierre. *The Arctic Grail: The Quest for the Northwest Passage and the North Pole 1818–1909.* New York: Penguin, 1988.

Bixby, William. *Track of the Bear.* New York: David McKay, 1965.

Bockstoce, John R. *Whales, Ice, and Men: The History of Whaling in the Western Arctic.* Seattle: University of Washington Press, 1986.

Brower, Charles D. *Fifty Years Below Zero: A Lifetime of Adventure in the Far North.* New York: Dodd, Mead, 1942.

Carpenter, Frank. *Alaska: Our Northern Wonderland.* Garden City, NY: Doubleday, Page, 1923. Chapter 26 available at http://www.alaskool.org/projects/reindeer/history/carpenter1928/CarpenterDeerMeat.html.

Cocke, Albert K. "Dr. Samuel J. Call." *Alaska Journal,* summer 1974.

Ellis, Richard. *Men and Whales.* New York: Random House, 1993.

Grosvener, Gilbert H. "Reindeer in Alaska." *National Geographic,* April 1903.

Institute of Social, Economic, and Government Research. "Alaska Reindeer Industry: The Early Period, 1892–1932." http://www.alaskool.org/projects/reindeer/history/iser1969/RDEER_2.html.

Jackson, Dr. Sheldon. *Annual Report on the Introduction of Domestic Reindeer into Alaska, 1898.* Washington, D.C., Government Printing Office, 1899.

Kane, Elisha Kent. *Arctic Explorations: An Account of the Second Grinnell Expedition in Search of Sir John Franklin.* New York: Arno Press, 1974.

Kroll, C. Douglas. *Commodore Ellsworth P. Bertholf: First Commandant of the Coast Guard.* Annapolis, MD: Naval Institute Press, 2002.

Log of the *Alexander.* New Bedford Whaling Museum, New Bedford, MA.

McKinley, President William. Special Message to Congress, January 17, 1899.

Murphy, Jim. *Gone A-Whaling: The Lure of the Sea and the Hunt for the Great Whale.* New York: Clarion, 1998.

Report of the Cruise of the U.S. Revenue Cutter Bear *and the Overland Expedition for the Relief of the Whalers in the Arctic Ocean, from November 27, 1897, to September 13, 1898.* Washington, DC: Government Printing Office, 1899.

Sandell, David. *The Bear.* Unpublished Manuscript.

Sandler, Martin W. *Trapped in Ice: An Amazing True Whaling Adventure.* New York: Scholastic, 2006.

Starbuck, Alexander. *History of the American Whale Fishery.* New York: Castle, 1991.

Taliaferro, John. *In a Far Country: The True Story of a Mission, a Marriage, a Murder, and the Remarkable Reindeer Rescue of 1898*. New York: PublicAffairs, 2006.

Tilton, George Fred. *"Cap'n George Fred" Himself*. Edgartown, MA: Dukes County Historical Society, 1969.

Wead, Frank W. *Gales, Ice and Men: A Biography of the Steam Barkentine* Bear. New York: Dodd, Mead, 1937.

Photography Credits

Index

Acknowledgments

I am grateful to Candlewick Press's Mary Lee Donovan for sharing my enthusiasm for this story. A large debt of gratitude is also owed to maritime curator Michael Dyer, librarian Laura Pereira, and curator of photography Michael Lapides of the New Bedford Whaling Museum for their valuable assistance. I am most appreciative of the help I received from Katherine Worten and from Carol Sandler, who, as always, were a constant source of encouragement. And I wish to thank Dianna Russo Glazer and Sherry Fatla for the volume's beautiful design and Alexandra Redmond for the meticulous way in which every fact in this book was checked and authenticated. Finally, there are not words adequate enough to express what Hilary Van Dusen has brought to this book. If this story has been brought to life in the way it deserves, it is, in great measure, due not only to her expert editing but also to the manner in which she has shaped this volume and guided its author. Thanks, Hilary.